MW00717615

Neither Male Nor Female Workbook

by
R. S. "Bud" Miller, D.D.
Publisher
Betty Miller, D.M.
Author

www.Bible.com

Overcoming Life Series

Christ Unlimited — P.O. Box 850 — Dewey, AZ 86327   USA

Unless otherwise indicated, all Scripture quotations are taken from the <u>King James Version of the Holy Bible</u> (KJV).

<u>Overcoming Life Series:</u>

<u>Neither Male Nor Female Workbook</u>

ISBN 1-57149-013-2

Copyright (c) 1995/2004

R. S. "Bud" and Betty Miller

P. O. Box 850

Dewey, Arizona 86327

Published by

Christ Unlimited Publishing

P. O. Box 850

Dewey, Arizona 86327

Publisher: Pastor R. S. "Bud" Miller

Contents

Personal Introduction

A lack of education will not hinder anyone from taking this course, and a doctor's degree will not help. However, one requirement that is necessary for this course to benefit the student is a <u>total commitment</u> to God. The Holy Spirit is our teacher, and we can learn if we come to God as little children. Being hungry to know God is a necessary prerequisite in order for this course to be of help.

If any of us are to receive truth, we must seek God, who is truth, with our whole hearts. We must seek Jesus first, then the knowledge of His Word will be revealed to us. Therefore, we want to emphasize once again the need to become as "a little child" in our approach to learning God's Word (Matt. 18:1-4; Jer. 29:13).

We need to come humbly before God, asking Him to remove any "know-it-all" attitudes, in order to be teachable. By laying down everything we thought we knew, we give God a chance to correct things we have believed that were wrong. Then we can begin to live the overcoming lives that God intended for His children to experience.

This course, the <u>Overcoming Life Series</u>, is made up of nine books and workbooks taken from our first published book, <u>How To Overcome Through the Christ Unlimited</u>. That book, given to us under the anointing of the Holy Spirit, covers most of the basic things a Christian needs to know to get started on a victorious, overcoming walk with the Lord.

Christ Unlimited — P.O. Box 850 — Dewey, AZ 86327   USA

We have purposely kept this course simple for the average Christian who needs help in understanding how to study the Word and how to sort out principles and concepts when he, or she, reads the Bible; however, it also is for the seminary student. In addition, it is designed for students who desire to use it as a correspondence course. They can learn from it, even if they are totally alone and without a human teacher. The Holy Spirit always is there to teach us as we study about His Word.

On the other hand, groups with a teacher, or moderator, also can use this course to advantage. Our prayer is that however this course is taken, each student will complete it a different person and be conformed more into the image of Christ our Lord.

Bud and Betty Miller

Neither Male Nor Female Workbook

Section One

"What Is True Submission?"

Christ Unlimited — P.O. Box 850 — Dewey, AZ 86327   USA

Neither Male Nor Female Workbook
Section One: "What Is True Submission?"
Expository Introduction

[Author's Note: This workbook is the seventh in the <u>Overcoming Life Series</u>, which includes nine books and workbooks. Lessons also have supplementary material. Answers are provided at the end of each workbook and do not have to be the exact wording in many cases. The student simply needs to make sure that he, or she, has caught the concept or principle from the Word of God.]

The text, or the basis for the three lessons in this workbook is Galatians 3:28:

There is neither Jew nor Greek, there is neither bond nor free, there is <u>neither male nor female</u>: for ye are all one in Christ Jesus.

What does the term, "neither male nor female," mean in the above verse? When the writers of the Bible spoke of "man," it usually was a generic term, meaning <u>mankind</u>, which also means "men and women," or "male and female." The "Adamic man" is <u>both</u> male and female (Gen. 5:2). All males and females, throughout the ages, were born in a "fallen" state due to Adam's sin, because the entire human race was in Adam when he sinned.

For as in Adam all die, even so in Christ shall all be made alive.

                                                1 Corinthians 15:22

Christ Unlimited — P.O. Box 850 — Dewey, AZ 86327   USA

In Peter's first letter to the Christians scattered throughout Asia Minor, he wrote about the proper attitudes of women to their husbands and made it clear that the heart attitude is what is important, not the outward appearance. In so writing, he told the women that it was the "hidden man of the heart" that should be meek and quiet and of great price in the eyes of God. If men and women are not counted as "man" to God, why would Peter have said "the hidden <u>man</u> of the heart" when he was speaking specifically to women?

> But let it be the hidden man of the heart, in that which is not corruptible, even the ornament of a meek and quiet spirit, which is in the sight of God of great price. For after this manner in the old time the holy women also, who trusted in God, adorned themselves, being in subjection unto their own husbands.
>
> 1 Peter 3:4,5

When God looks upon a person's spirit, He looks at the heart and makes no distinction because of race, class, culture, sex, or denominational beliefs. Therefore, being in Christ, we are restored to life free from the penalty of sin. Believers are to relate to one another on a spiritual basis, not on any natural distinction. The spiritual basis is that we are brothers and sisters adopted through Christ (Rom. 8:15), and we have the same Father — God (1 Cor. 10:17). Also, God refers to His children in the Bible as "sons," which includes both male or female (Rom. 8:14 and 1 John 3:1,2, which obviously are referring to <u>all</u> believers).

Even in the world, until the past quarter century, mankind was referred to in generic terms as "he." In many areas, this is still true. Until the '70s and '80s, when we began to hear a lot about "the liberation of women," no one considered anything wrong with this. Then that movement began to insist on using female pronouns as well as male when referring to mankind. The Women's Lib movement is not based on biblical principles and is a counterfeit of God's true liberation of women.

When Eve ate the forbidden fruit and enticed Adam to sin with her, one of the consequences for women was the loss of equality with men, as men were to rule over women instead of men and women ruling together (Gen. 3:16). However, when Jesus came as sinless Man and died as Messiah on the cross for us, all things were restored <u>positionally</u>. In actuality, the restoration of man (men and women) began to take place then. Or, to put it another way, all those who receive Jesus as Savior receive restoration as Sons of God, but not all of us <u>walk</u> in that restoration. The curse upon women was lifted. Women no longer have to receive pain in childbirth nor are they inferior to man with him ruling over them. Women were now restored to their original place and plan God had for all of His "sons."

Adam was the head of the first race of mankind; and, Jesus is the Head of the last race, the adopted children of God. God only sees two races — the Adamic race (all natural-born mankind) and His children through Jesus (all of those born of the Spirit).

And so it is written, The first man Adam was made a living soul: the last Adam was made a quickening spirit... The first man is of the earth, earthy: the second man is the Lord from heaven. As is the earthy, such are they also that are earthy: and as is the heavenly, such are they also that are heavenly. And as we have borne the image of the earthy, we shall also bear the image of the heavenly.

1 Corinthians 15:45,47-49

As we discussed in the <u>Healing of Spirit, Soul, and Body Workbook</u>, restoration for us begins at conversion, continues through the process of sanctification, and ends at the Resurrection with the transformation of our natural bodies into new ones (1 Cor. 15:42-44). Although we do not <u>see</u> all things restored at this time, "legally" in the spiritual realm, they have been.

Submission Operates on Many Levels

One of the things God requires of His children is that they learn to submit to authority, and that applies to men as well as women. <u>Submission</u> is a voluntary giving up of your will for someone else's, while <u>surrender</u> means being forced to give up. Submission is a heart attitude, a loving agreement and yielded spirit to do what another asks of us. Proper submission begins for believers in submitting our wills to that of the Father. In a society run by fallen man (and woman) under Satan's influence, submission has been out of balance in two extremes:

1. Some people are so independent and self-willed that they refuse to submit to any authority.

2. Others submit without discernment to every dictate of those who are stronger than themselves physically, emotionally, or spiritually.

The proper balance is submission through the leadership of the Holy Spirit, and submission operates on many levels.

In the home, submission is supposed to be <u>mutual</u> between husband and wife (Eph. 5:21; Rom. 12:10). On the other hand, the husband is to be the head of the house (Eph. 5:23). With the man's position of authority, there also comes a great responsibility. The husband is told to protect and lovingly care for his wife, even to the point of laying down his life for her as Jesus did the Church (Eph. 5:25-29). And the wife is to be as submissive to her husband as the Church is supposed to be to Christ (Eph. 5:24). It is easy for a woman to yield to a husband who loves her as Christ loves the Church.

However, the wife's submission to the husband does have limits, and those limits involve where God's authority begins and the husband's stops (Matt. 22:37). For example, if a husband asks his wife to lie, steal, commit adultery, or other things that are against the will of God, then her submission to him in those areas ends. God's authority is the ultimate authority.

In Acts 5, we have a classic example of a wife who should <u>not</u> have submitted to her husband in a certain matter. Ananias lied to the Holy Spirit and to the apostles, and he died. If Sapphira had not submitted to Ananias and also lied, her life would have been spared.

The story of Abigail and Nabal in 1 Samuel 25:4-42 is an example of a wife who did not obey her husband when his command was wrong and against the will of the Lord. In this case, he died but her life was spared.

Should a husband ask something immoral or ungodly of a wife, she should still respond in a loving and respectful manner even when denying his request. When husband and wife argue and fight, it is as though they were tearing their own flesh (Eph. 5:29). Solomon wrote in Proverbs 21:9 that it would be better to live in a corner on top of a house than in a large house with a "brawling" woman and the same is true of men. A husband and wife should edify (build up) one another, praying for each other to do the will of the Father (1 Pet. 3:1-12). Marriage partners are to give 100 percent to the marriage, not the 50 percent the world says they are to give.

Christian women experience two "marriages" in which they have two "heads," one is their natural husband and one is Jesus, Husband of the Bride of Christ, of which they are a part. The husband is to be the priest of the home, but he is not the spiritual head. The spiritual head of both husband and wife is the Lord. So if the Lord leads a woman to move in a spiritual gift during a service, she need not first ask her husband for permission. However, out of respect for whoever is leading the service, and out of submission to the proper church authority, she should be sensitive to designated leadership before ministering in a gift.

Christ Unlimited — P.O. Box 850 — Dewey, AZ 86327   USA

If the husband was the spiritual head of a woman, she would have to go to him to repent. However, when a woman sins, she goes to the Lord. She does not go to her husband for forgiveness — unless the sin was against him personally. Women who are unequally yoked (their husbands are unbelievers) still have their husbands as heads of the marriage and Christ as spiritual Head. Single women who are believers have only one Head, Jesus. An Old Testament example of a single woman whose obedience to the will of God saved her household is Rahab (Josh. 2:1-24, 6:21-25).

Authority Carries Great Responsibility

In examining Church authority, we find there are two aspects to God's order. He requires submission to His designated authorities (Heb. 13:17); but at the same time, He instructed His ministers not to "lord it" over the flock or use them for personal gain or benefit (Ez. 34:2-10; 1 Pet. 5:3). With authority comes responsibility and accountability. Leadership is to be by example as much as by command (1 Pet. 3:5), and they must be submitted to God.

If wives understood how much their husbands are going to be accountable in regard to their husbands' treatment of them, it would be much easier for them to be forgiving and compassionate. On the other hand, many husbands would be more loving and protective heads of their families if they realized they are going to have to give an account of their stewardship when they face God.

The principles of designated authority and willing submission to that authority was designed by God to set life in order for the benefit of His people. However, both those who walk in authority and those who submit to authority must have the right attitudes, or God's system does not work. Because the Adamic race does not walk in spiritual love and understanding, the authorities set over us do not always do everything perfectly, and the natural soul is full of rebellion. Those two facts about the world and natural man do not, however, mean God's principles of authority and submission are not still in effect.

Each believer is accountable for his attitudes, whether he is in authority or in a place where submission is required. Every person has someone over him, and will have someone over him, throughout eternity. Man was not created to ever be his own authority.

In the Church, leadership is commissioned to watch over the souls of believers (Heb. 13:17). Authority in the Church and in civil government brings order in the local church and in the world. We are to submit to those authorities even when we believe they are making mistakes <u>as long as they are not moving against the explicit Word of God</u>. God will honor our submission, as He will honor the submission of wives to husbands, even when husbands are making mistakes.

Believers are specifically instructed not to correct an elder (1 Tim. 5:1,2). In other words, church members do not have the responsibility nor the right to correct those in the five-fold ministries. God will correct them through an equal, or directly Himself. Certainly if there is sin in a leader's life, it should not be ignored. It should be dealt with in a scriptural manner, not openly rebuked with a disrespectful attitude. If the corrected elder does not heed God's correction, then God knows how to deal with that minister so the flock is not brought under bondage. God can change the hearts of church leadership and of husbands, so we need to pray for our "heads" in every area of life.

When there is a problem, it always is a good idea to examine oneself first. We need to make certain we are not the ones who need to change. If a minister is at fault, God will use a higher authority to correct him, or someone of equal authority, not someone of lower authority.

A key scripture dealing with submission is James 4:7:

Submit yourselves therefore to God....

We are to submit to God, and the rest of that verse says to **resist the devil, and he will flee from you.** Many of us are guilty at times of submitting to the things the devil runs over us with and resisting the things God wants us to do.

A good question to ask the Lord each night before going to bed is, "Lord, is there any sin I committed today that I need to take care of?"

The Holy Spirit might bring to our memories some wrong attitudes, words that should not have been spoken, or something we should have done and did not do. We need to repent of those things and resist the devil in those areas. Then, God has promised us that the devil will flee from us.

Other areas of submission Christians are instructed to observe include children to parents (Eph. 6:1-3), the younger to the elder (1 Pet. 5:5), everyone to governmental authorities (Rom. 13:1-5; 1 Pet. 2:13,14), and servants to their masters (Eph. 6:5-8; 1 Tim. 6:1,2). Today, we would say employees to their employers.

The old saying that a person cannot be a good leader until he first learns to be a good follower is very true. Women who feel led to any type of leadership role should first learn to submit to whatever constituted authority is over them.

There has been much discussion in the past few years about "Jezebel spirits," and some people have gone to extremes with this. Jezebel and Absalom spirits are types taken from the Old Testament. In reading about their lives, we can see that the evil traits that were in them are still at work today in others. Every woman with a strong spirit or personality is not a Jezebel. Also, men can be influenced by the same controlling spirits. The key is whether or not authority is being usurped. A strong woman, called by God and submitted to Jesus <u>and</u> her husband (if she is married) is not Jezebel when she ministers, handles a career, or her home. She is simply carrying out her assignment from God.

On the other hand, a "Jezebel spirit" can be recognized by the following traits:

1. They refuse God's Word through the leadership.
2. They blame others for their problems.
3. They use their gifts or goods to manipulate others.
4. They use fear or threats to control others.

5. They are prideful.

6. They want their own ways all of the time.

7. They use others to stir up trouble against leadership.

8. They also at times work behind the scenes using others to do their dirty work.

9. They are committing a form of spiritual witchcraft and idolatry.

These traits can be recognized in the story of how Jezebel ruled her husband, Ahab, and tried to destroy Elijah and God's other prophets of the time through her evil rebellion (1 Kings 18-21).

This same spirit is still in the Church today seeking to destroy God's work. We are not to tolerate it (Rev. 2:20-23).

Men can also have this spirit. If they move to usurp authority from a boss or pastor, then they are under the influence of a "Jezebel spirit." If he continues to walk in this, he will also come under an "Absalom spirit" and begin to actively move toward taking over the role of the man or woman over him; just as Absalom did in regard to David's authority (2 Sam. 15).

True submission on a woman's part does not require her to be a "door mat;" however, it does require her to keep a proper heart attitude to all authority over her. A submissive spirit is just the opposite of a "Jezebel spirit."

Lesson for Section One

[Author's Note: All Scripture references that answer these questions have been given. Please do not look at the answer pages until you have answered the questions in your own words. This is an expository lesson to help you learn.]

I. The Role of Women in General

    A. The true liberation of women occurred when Jesus died on the cross and cancelled the curse against them.

        1. "Women's Lib" is a _____ of the true liberation of women.

        2. When were women placed under dominance of their husbands?_____

        Reference: **Genesis 3:16**

    B. When the Bible speaks of <u>man</u>, the general reference is to both _____ and _____, who together constitute mankind.

    References: **Genesis 1:27, 5:2; Ephesians 2:15**

        1. The "Adamic man" then is both male and _____.

        2. All men and women have been in a fallen state due to the _____ of Adam.

        Reference: **1 Cor. 15:45-50; 1 Pet. 3:4**

C. God makes no distinction between His new creatures because of race, class, culture, or _____.
Reference: **Galatians 3:28; 2 Corinthians 5:16,17**

D. God uses both men and women who have committed themselves to Him and who are _____ to Him.

1. Submission in the home is to be a mutual submission to one another, but with the man as the recognized _____.
Reference: **Ephesians 5:21-23**

2. _____ should be the rule of the home as well as in the church.

Be kindly affectioned one to another with brotherly love; in honour preferring one another.

Romans 12:10

II. Attitudes of Submission

A. Wives are to be submitted to their husbands as the Church is submitted to _____.
Reference: **Ephesians 5:24**

1. What exception is there to a wife's submission?

_____

Christ Unlimited — P.O. Box 850 — Dewey, AZ 86327   USA

2. Submission to _____ must supercede submission to husbands or any other earthly authority.
Reference: Acts 4:17-20

   a. What Old Testament wife was right in her refusal to submit to her husband's orders? _____
   Reference: 1 Samuel 25

   b. What New Testament wife would have lived if she had refused to submit to her husband? _____
   Reference: Acts 5:1-11

3. Who is the spiritual Head of all Christian women, married or single? _____
   a. A woman's obedience to God can make a way for those of her _____ to be saved and delivered.
   b. A single woman in the Old Testament whose obedience to God's will saved her household was _____.
   Reference: Joshua 6:25

B. Submission can be out of balance and go to extremes.
   1. One extreme is _____ and refusing to submit to any authority.
   Reference: Isaiah 30:1,9
   2. The other extreme is to submit to _____ kind of authority, regardless of the circumstances.

3. Submitting to the _____ of the church will bring the proper order in local congregations.

III. The Reason for Authority and Submission

A. Submission to church authority brings about _____ in the church.

Reference: First Corinthians 14:40

1. Those in authority should rule in love and service and by _____.

Reference: 1 Peter 5:3

2. Believers are told to _____ those in authority who are responsible for the souls of those under them.

Obey them that have the rule over you, and submit yourselves: for they watch for your souls, as they that must give account, that they may do it with joy, and not with grief: for that is unprofitable for you.

Hebrews 13:17

B. Believers also are told to be _____ to another.

Likewise, ye younger, submit yourselves unto the elder. Yea, all of you be subject one to another, and be clothed with humility: for God resisteth the proud, and giveth grace to the humble.

1 Peter 5:5

1. The younger believers are to submit to the _____.
   Reference: 1 Peter 5:5

2. We are instructed not only not to rebuke an elder but also not to receive an _____ against him unless it is before two or three witnesses.
   Reference: 1 Timothy 5:1,19

Overcoming Life Memory Verse

The suggested memory verse for this section are:

Submit yourselves therefore to God. Resist the devil, and he will flee from you. . . . Humble yourselves in the sight of the Lord, and he shall lift you up.

James 4:7,10

Review Outline, Section One

I. **Bible Teaching Concerning Women**

   A. God's Word teaches that real freedom for all women and all mankind comes only through Jesus (Gen. 1:27, 5:2; 1 Cor. 15:21,22, 45-50).

   1. Both men and women were under the penalty of spiritual death because of sin (Gen. 2:17, 3:3,22).

   2. Both men and women were redeemed from this penalty at Calvary (Gal. 3:13,14).

   3. Both men and women are liberated to the original status God intended <u>when they become born again</u> (John 3:3-7; Gal. 3:26-29).

   4. Both men and women, who are born again, have Jesus as their spiritual Head (Eph. 5:23,24).

   B. The Women's Liberation movement is a counterfeit of real freedom in Christ.

   1. In actuality, this movement has brought women into more bondage and stress than previously by:

      a. Opening the door for more competition with men.

      b. Enticing women to usurp authority as a "right."

      c. Downgrading homemaking as inferior.

      d. Taking on responsibilities she is not equipped to handle.

   2. The result has been that many women have fallen into the "superwoman complex:" trying to be as good in the market place as men and still be a perfect wife, mother, and housekeeper.

C. In Christ, there is neither male nor female (Gal. 3:27,28).

  1. In Him, both men and women are new creatures (Gal. 6:15).

  2. Neither born again men nor women are to regard one another after the flesh, which means no segregation according to:

    a. Gender

    b. Race, or nationality

    c. Class

    d. Culture

    Reference: **Romans 8**

  3. Christians are to see one another through spiritual eyes (2 Cor. 5:16,17).

  4. God accepts all those who will receive Him without regard to race, class, gender, or culture (Acts 10:34,35).

    a. He equips those He calls and sends including women (Eph. 4:1-7).

    b. The fact that "sons of God" (Gal. 4:4-7), "priests and kings" (Rev. 1:6), and other terms such as "Bride of Christ/Body of Christ" are used of both men and women shows that in the Kingdom of God, men and women are equal in all things.

      1) God sees the <u>hearts</u> of people and chooses them for office accordingly, not by any other criteria.

      2) Obedience and faithfulness are what matter to God, not one's sex.

  5. Inequality of the sexes occurred at the fall of Adam and

Eve (Gen. 3:16). Although both sexes sinned, Eve "enticed" Adam (Gen. 3:6).

   a. Before the fall, there was equality between Adam and Eve — a partnership, not domination (Gen. 5:2).

   b. The command to have dominion, subdue, and replenish the earth was given to both Adam and Eve (Gen.1:27,28).

   c. True equality was restored at Calvary <u>in Christ</u>, not by the world's system (2 Cor. 5:17-21).

II. Principles of Submission and Headship

A. Basics of Submission (Eph. 5:21-33).

   1. <u>Submission</u> means "to yield" or "to set oneself under."

      a. Submission is an attitude that comes to a loving agreement with those set over a person.

      b. Surrender simply is giving up, or resigning to authority, because that authority is stronger or a greater force.

      c. God wants submission that is willing, not surrender that comes by force.

   2. Both men and women, who are born again, are called to submit to Jesus, subordinating their wills to His, as He did to the Father (John 6:38).

   3. All believers should prefer one another, including wives and husbands in the home (Rom. 12:10; Eph. 5:21).

   4. Submission must be balanced, according to the wisdom of God (James 3:13-18).

      a. The Holy Spirit must be the true leader (Rom. 8:14).

    b. Legalism, dictatorship, or permissiveness must be avoided by husbands if they are to be true heads of their homes.

  5. Single women are not under any earthly headship. Their head is Jesus (Rom. 7:4). They are, however, to be submitted to all earthly delegated authorities.

B. Guidelines for Submission in Marriage

  1. A woman's first submission is to the Lord even as the Lord's call on Mary's life superceded Joseph's right to her (Luke 1:38).

  2. In marriage, women are subject to their husbands' headships (Eph. 5:24).

    a. Submission to her husband reflects a woman's submission to the Lord.

    b. Wives are not to obey their husbands in matters that are against the Word and will of God (Matt. 22:37-39).

      1) Wives must be sure something is against God's will before not obeying their husbands.

      2) Both wives and husbands must be willing to be corrected (1 Pet. 3:1-12).

      3) Wives and husbands must pray for each other in order to stay in the proper attitudes of love and respect. (Eph. 5:33).

  3. Sometimes, however, the Lord speaks or gives direction through the wife and not the husband (Gen. 21:10-12). The Holy Spirit generally will not override a husband.

C. Guidelines for Submission to Elders

(Elders are those who are wise, more mature, or in positions of church and spiritual authority — Heb. 13:17.)

1. Elders, both men and women, are to be respected and not rebuked or accused unscripturally (1 Tim. 5:1,2,19).

2. Elder women can teach younger men and women (1 Pet. 5:5; Titus 2:3-5).

3. Also, in this situation, legalism, dictatorship, or permissiveness on the part of elders must be avoided as there is greater judgment on leaders (James 3:1).

4. True shepherds lead by love and example (1 Pet. 5:3).

Christ Unlimited — P.O. Box 850 — Dewey, AZ 86327   USA

Review Outline Quiz, Section One

1. What is the Christian's final authority on any subject?

    _____

2. Real freedom for women comes through _____

    _____

3. In Christ, there is neither _____ nor _____

    _____.

4. What counts with God more than one's gender?

    _____ and _____

5. What criteria does God use for choosing those to serve Him in leadership positions?

    _____

6. Who must be the true leader of both men and women?

    _____

7. A woman's first submission is to _____.

8. Submission means to yield by _____,
    while surrender means to yield by _____
    _____.

9. Both husbands and wives should be willing to receive _____
    _____.

10. True shepherds lead their flocks by _____
    and_____.

Neither Male Nor Female Workbook
Section Two
"Woman's Role in the Church"

Christ Unlimited — P.O. Box 850 — Dewey, AZ 86327   USA

Neither Male Nor Female Workbook
Section Two: "Woman's Role in the Church"
Expository Introduction

Looking at **Galatians 3:28** shows us the mind of God about the role of women in the church.

There is neither Jew nor Greek, there is neither bond nor free, there is neither male nor female: for ye are all one in Christ.

Galatians 3:28

Since the Lord looks at the hearts of men and women, He uses any willing and committed vessel to do His work. God does not base His decision on gender, race, or status. He uses both men and women in the five-fold ministry offices in the order of the Church.

The modern-day church as a whole has not recognized these five offices today, but has, for the most part, only acknowledged the office of evangelist and pastor. The apostle has been reduced to a missionary, while the office of teacher has deteriorated to a Sunday-school teacher, and the prophet does not even exist except as recorded in the pages of the Bible. All of these offices still are valid today and part of the restoration of the Church that is occurring now is the reinstating of these offices in the Body of Christ.

In fact, the current emphasis has been on the office of the prophet and the prophetic movement, which will then usher in the apostolic giftings. These five-fold ministries are His gifts to help bring the Church to maturity. Dr. Bill Hamon has some excellent books that will help bring understanding in regard to the prophetic movement. They are recommended reading.[1]

Ephesians 4:4-16 tells us why Jesus gave ministry "gifts" to men.

There is one body, and one Spirit, even as ye are called in one hope of your calling; One Lord, one faith, one baptism, One God and Father of all, who is above all, and through all, and in you all. But unto everyone of us is given grace according to the measure of the gift of Christ. Wherefore he saith, When he ascended up on high, he led captivity captive, and gave gifts unto men. (Now that he ascended, what is it but that he also descended first into the lower parts of the earth? He that descended is the same also that ascended up far above all heavens, that he might fill all things. And he gave some, apostles; and some, prophets; and some, evangelists; and some, pastors and teachers: For the perfecting of the saints, for the work of the ministry, for the edifying of the body of Christ: Till we all come in the unity of the faith, and of the knowledge of the Son of God, unto a perfect man, unto the measure of the stature of the fulness of Christ: That we henceforth be no more children, tossed to and fro, and carried about with every wind of doctrine, by the sleight of men, and cunning craftiness, whereby they lie in wait to deceive; But speaking the truth in love, may grow up into him in all things, which is the head, even Christ: From whom the whole body fitly joined together and compacted by that which every joint supplieth, according to the effectual working in the measure of every part, maketh increase of the body unto the edifying of itself in love.

In those verses, men and women are referred to in general terms as "man," meaning mankind. Jesus is the Head, and we are to be His Body measuring up to the fullness of His stature, making a "perfect man." Many places where "he" or "his" is written in the Bible, it is in reference to both men and women.

In Ephesians 4:5-7, the Apostle Paul wrote that there is one body, Spirit, Lord, faith, baptism, and God and Father of all. He did not divide the Body into different races, classes, cultures, or genders. Therefore, women are included in the category of the "gifts" of Jesus to men. Jesus sets those in the five-fold offices into their places, because He is Head of the Church. Not all men or women who have the title of minister are truly called by God. Many have assumed the role for various reasons, but God does not recognize them. He only commissions those of His choosing and sets them in His five-fold ministry offices.

The five offices are: apostle, prophet, evangelist, pastor, teacher. They are <u>ordained</u> by God, and their purpose is to bring the entire Body into maturity, according to the above verses in Ephesians. Sometimes, these offices are also ordained by earthly organizations. However, not all of God's ministers are acknowledged by man-made organizations. But the ordination by Jesus is what counts. The spiritual qualifications of those called, according to Scripture, are:

1. They must be called of God.

2. They are to be tested and spiritually mature.

3. They will be empowered and gifted by the Holy Spirit to fulfill their callings.

4. They must know the Word of God.

5. They must be ordained of God.

The Greek word for ordain means "to appoint, to set apart, to decide, and judge." When God ordains someone, He has made a judgment on a life. He judges one worthy to receive His position of authority to minister to His sheep. His chosen ministers are His "gifts" to the Body of Christ. Every person selected for the five-fold ministry will have been tested by God and also by the devil before his, or her, appointment. God tests by giving His people choices to do what is right and what is according to His Word. The devil tests by tempting with circumstances to keep us from moving in God. Those who pass the tests are qualified by God.

It is as important for a person to get God's timing on when to move out in ministry as it is to know his calling. He must also have God's plan as to <u>where</u> to go. Some people, who entered the ministry as a career, are ordained legally. However, they were not ordained by God. Also, people are in the ministry who were not called by God, but who were "called" by their own desires, their parents, or by others.

Others are called but have strayed along the way. The end result will be death of their ministries, sooner or later. Recently, we have seen some instances of this exposed in the news media. Those who refuse to repent of sin and be cleaned up will end up shipwrecked (1 Tim. 1:18,19). They must stay submitted to the will of the Father to fulfill their calling. Some do not keep their home lives in order, and "death" of another kind will result —divorce or children in trouble. However, even if these ministers fail, their callings and giftings are irrevocable (Rom. 11:29). God does not take their positions from them. The devil robs and destroys their ministries because of their own weaknesses or sins. If such a person does not fulfill the calling, he will have to give an account to God in the Judgment for the lack of results of their callings or gifts.

Apostles and Prophets: the Foundation

Jesus Christ is allegorically referred to as the Chief Cornerstone in the building or house known as the Holy Temple of the Lord. God's people are "living stones" making up that House, while the apostles and prophets make up the foundation of the building. They are the teachers and leaders of the entire Body of Christ.

Now therefore ye are no more strangers and foreigners, but fellow-citizens with the saints, and of the household of God; And are built upon the foundation of the apostles and prophets, Jesus Christ himself being the chief corner stone; In whom all the building fitly framed together groweth unto an holy temple in the Lord: In whom ye also are builded together for an habitation of God through the Spirit.

Ephesians 2:19-22

Christ Unlimited — P.O. Box 850 — Dewey, AZ 86327   USA

Because of the leadership and ministry of the apostles and prophets, they are first called to minister to the Lord.

He ordained twelve, that they should <u>be with him</u>, and that he might send them forth to preach.

Mark 3:14

Out of being <u>with Him</u> flows ministry to other people (John 15:5,7-9). Ministry in reality should be an overflow of a fellowship with the Lord. Too many ministers feel they should be ministered to rather than giving to others. The way up in the Kingdom is down, according to Matthew 20:25-28, which says the "greatest" in the Kingdom is one who is the servant of all, not one who wants to be served. To gain promotion in God's Kingdom, the key is to be faithful in whatever office a person is first placed. If someone is not faithful in the little things, he will not be faithful in the greater things (Luke 16:10).

The first office mentioned, the apostle, should have all of the qualifications of the other offices and be able to fill those offices if necessary. Most apostles have usually already functioned in the other offices as God has used those positions to train them for the apostolic giftings. In fact, some of the early apostles were filling the role of deacons as well as being apostles until the Lord led them to elect the first deacons (Acts 6:1-5).

<u>Diakonos</u>, translated "deacons," means "one who runs errands, ministers or serves, or helps many." The qualifications are listed in 1 Timothy 3:1-13. Today, this office is considered "the ministry of

helps." Elders comes from the Greek word presbuteros, meaning "one who is spiritually mature." There are two types of elders mentioned in the Bible: 1) older men and women, who are to be treated with respect and who are to teach younger Christians, and 2) an office in the church, which involves ruling and teaching. Christians are told not to rebuke an elder or to receive an accusation against one unless it is done carefully by scriptural instruction. Also, there should be at least two or three witnesses to his crime or sin (1 Tim. 5:19). Another church office that is not one of the five-fold offices, but an administrative role, is bishop. The Greek word is episcopos, which means "one who oversees, or a superintendent" (Phil. 1:1; Titus 1:5-9; 1 Tim. 3:1-7).

Other aspects of the office of apostle are:

*To establish the Kingdom life of God in the Church

*One sent from God as a special messenger (Gal. 1:1). The Greek word translated apostle actually means "one sent forth."

*Those anointed and gifted as apostles operate in special miracles and signs and wonders. "Handkerchiefs or aprons" that had been next to Paul's body brought healing and deliverance (Acts 19:11). Peter walked through town, and everyone that his shadow touched was healed (Acts 5:15,16).

*The fruit of the Spirit has been perfected in the lives of apostles, and they accomplish mighty deeds (2 Cor. 12:12). An apostle will be patient and not easily upset. The Apostle Paul's life had been perfected in such a way that by the time he wrote to the Corinthian Christians (1 Cor. 4:15,16, 11:1), he could say: Follow me as I follow Christ.

*Apostles come into churches and straighten out problems, as well as ordain elders (Titus 1:5; Acts 14:23).

*Apostles can be missionaries, but not all missionaries are apostles.

The next office mentioned in **Ephesians 4:11** is that of prophet. There are modern-day prophets, although not all of Christendom recognizes them. The prophet or prophetess will preach or expound the Word of God and also speak divine utterances at the unction of the Holy Spirit. Old Testament prophets largely proclaimed messages of salvation and glory to be accomplished in the future. The Old Testament prophet also was used to warn God's people of impending judgments when they willfully sinned.

The New Testament prophets were used to make known that which already had been accomplished, plus foretelling the purposes of God for the future. John the Baptist was the first New Testament prophet, and Jesus was the second. Jesus was the sum total of all of the five offices. He simply divided the aspects of His ministry into five categories and scattered them among the entire Body, much as the Levites were seeded throughout Israel. Old Testament prophets were stoned if their prophetic words failed to come to pass as that revealed them to be false prophets (Deut. 18:20-22).

New Testament prophets are not to be considered false prophets if they make a mistake, but rather, they are to have their words judged or proved by the standard of God's Word and the gift of discernment in other prophets of God as to their accuracy (1 Cor. 14:29).

Christ Unlimited — P.O. Box 850 — Dewey, AZ 86327   USA

In Dr. Bill Hamon's book, <u>Prophets, Pitfalls, and Principles</u>, he describes the office of prophet as follows:[1]

"The ministry of the office of prophet is not a gift of the Holy Spirit, but a gift-extension of Christ Himself as the prophet. The five-fold ministry of the Church . . . is not an external endowment like a birthday present. Instead, it is an investment of Christ's mantle for the ministries of Jesus — a divine impartation of Christ's own nature, wisdom, and power for each particular kind of performance — whether apostle, prophet, pastor, teacher, or evangelist. All five, when moving in full maturity, represent Christ's full ministry to the Church. This is an extension of the headship of Christ to His Body, the Church."

Evangelists, Pastors, and Teachers

The evangelist essentially is the <u>messenger of the Gospel</u>. The word <u>gospel</u> means "good news." This news is the report of what Jesus did on the cross to reconcile man to God (2 Cor. 5:18-20). The evangelist's main job is to carry out the mission of "the Great Commission" (Mark 16:15-20), although every Christian has the responsibility of telling others about Christ whenever and wherever the Holy Spirit leads.

Examples of New Testament evangelists were Phillip and Barnabas. Signs and wonders always followed them wherever they ministered. They shared the salvation message, as well as that of baptisms and the provisions of deliverance from demons, speaking in other tongues, and the healing of the sick; in other words, "the basics of the faith" (Heb. 6:1,2). As they traveled, they knew because of Jesus' words recorded in **Mark 16:15-18** that they would be protected from poisonous food and beverages and even from deadly snakes, as Paul was on the island of Melita (Malta) after a shipwreck (Acts 28:1-6).

Since the Reformation, the main two offices in the Church have been pastor and evangelist. The other three offices have been restored to the Church in the past quarter of a century. (God had not removed them, but the Church ignored the other three offices.)

The office of pastor has remained through the ages. The Greek word for pastor is "poimen," which means shepherd. The pastor's main assignment is the feeding, protecting, and guiding of the sheep. The most important thing for pastors to remember is this: God owns the flock (Ezek. 34; Acts 20:28; 1 Pet. 5:1-4); they do not.

Pastors who are in the pastorate for their own gain or their own ambitions are "hirelings" who do not lay down their lives for the sheep (John 10:7-15).

On the other hand, pastors who do not distinguish their responsibilities from God's, will "burn-out," wear out physically, or have nervous breakdowns. It is very important to know what portion is the pastor's responsibility and what is the Lord's.

The five-fold office of teacher was restored to the Body of Christ in the '70s and '80s. For years, many Christians had considered the offices of pastor-teacher as one, or they thought that teacher referred to "Sunday-school teachers." But for His Endtime Church, God is restoring the five-fold offices in the fullness that Jesus intended and which operated in the early Church.

Someone called as a teacher usually has a different anointing and style than a pastor, although pastors sometimes "teach" instead of "preach." Teachers truly ordained of God will have special revelation and knowledge to make clear the teachings of God's Word (Acts 1:1; 2 Tim. 2:2). They impart life to their hearers by revelation knowledge and not by intellect (Gal. 1:11,12). Parables and allegories also accompany the function of teaching in the office of teacher even as they did Jesus' ministry (Mark 4:33,34).

Jesus was the master teacher, and as He expounded on God's Word, the people were able to understand the doctrines of God. God's teachers today have this same ability.

All of these offices, five-fold and administrative, were ordained by Jesus for these reasons:

*To take the message of the Kingdom to the world (Matt. 24:14)

*To bring the Body of Christ to maturity (Eph. 4:11-15)

*To have local churches operate in decency and order (1 Cor. 14:40).

Where there is chaos and confusion, you may be sure God is not being allowed to be the authority (1 Cor. 14:33).

Four Types of Church Order

There are four types of church order or government that we see in the world today with some mixtures between the types, but most of these are of man's devising and not of God's instruction. These have been developed over the past 500 years. They are:

*The episcopal government

*The presbytery government

*The congregational government

*The independent form of church government

The episcopal type of church government was adopted by the Episcopalians, Catholics, Anglicans, Lutherans, and United Methodists, as well as the various offshoots of Methodism — Nazarenes, Pilgrim Holiness, Wesleyan Methodist, and so forth. This means the administration, rules, and regulations come from a central governing board headed by a bishop, although delegates from various churches meet annually and vote on rules, regulations, and policies.

The presbytery form is used by the Presbyterian Church. This is a government in which elders ("presbyters") rule over the church. Many other churches, independent and non-denominational, have chosen this form of government. The elders choose pastors, tell them what to do, and "fire" them. This is not a Biblical form of government.

The congregational government was initiated when the United States was formed as a Republic with a democratic form of governing. Through the 20th century, we have become more and more a "democracy" instead of a republic. Socialistic, or liberal, trends have prevailed. In its church form, congregational means that the "sheep" run the church, as in Baptist denominations. The people vote the pastors in and out of service. Democracy may work in the world, but it is not God's choice for a form of government in His Church.

Christ Unlimited — P.O. Box 850 — Dewey, AZ 86327   USA

God's first choice is a <u>theocracy</u>, which means God ordains leaders (pastors), who will rule for Him so that, essentially, God is in charge through His Holy Spirit. Most <u>independent</u> churches today are functioning under this order. The proper governmental form to reflect this type of divine governing is for the pastor to be in charge with an advisory council of elders making up the "council of two or three witnesses" in which the Bible says security is found (Matt. 18:16; 2 Cor. 13:1).

Rationalism or "humanism" (the making of man into his own god and authority) have infiltrated the Church since the 18th century. Today, God is bringing order back into the Church. If the Holy Spirit truly has authority in a local body, a pastor will know who should take his place if he is moved by the Lord to some other place. <u>Voting for a new pastor is not scriptural</u>.

Now that we have discussed the true church offices and the true church order, we shall see how the Bible makes it clear that women have a place in His divine order of His Church government.

Women in the Five-Fold Ministry

God uses both men and women in His ministry offices. Both are to have submissive and aggressive traits according to the direction of the Holy Spirit. Women are to be aggressive against the enemy and in telling the good news through whatever office they hold. Laywomen also are to be aggressive against the enemy and in fulfilling the Great Commission in witnessing as the Lord leads

Christ Unlimited — P.O. Box 850 — Dewey, AZ 86327   USA

them. However, women in offices or as laypersons are <u>not</u> to be aggressive against their husbands or other constituted authority set over them in the church, the workplace, or civil governments.

Men and women are "the sons of God," as we discussed in the last section of this workbook. Men and women both are "the Bride of Christ," so that men are to be as submissive to Christ as women. In the Spirit, there is <u>neither male nor female</u> (Gal. 3:28). God made both men and women to have dominion and to subdue those things that are against the Kingdom of God (Gen. 1:27,28). Both men and women are created in God's image.

Women in the five-fold offices do not walk in their own authority — and neither do men — if they truly are called and ordained by Jesus. Both male and female five-fold office holders walk in the authority of Jesus. They are ambassadors of the King of kings, who speak for Him as the Holy Spirit gives them utterance.

As discussed in the last section, Jezebelic demons can influence men as well as women. The main characteristics of these spirits are the usurping of authority, not sexual enticement traits. Men in the five-fold office can usurp the authority of Jesus, if they are not careful. Then they open themselves up to Jezebelic spirits, and their motives can become those of self-as-god: pride, greed, ambition, and control. Both male and female traits come from God. His nature encompasses both of them. The prayer of Jesus in **Matthew 23:37** shows the nurturing ways of God. The Holy Spirit "mothers" and nurtures us if we will receive it. **Revelation 1:6** shows the male authority of God, as both men and women believers are "kings and priests" unto God.

Christ Unlimited — P.O. Box 850 — Dewey, AZ 86327   USA

Many men object to women in the ministry on the basis of some instructions Paul gave in his epistles. Like everything else in the Bible, however, doctrines should not be made out of one or two verses taken out of context. Scripture should be compared with scripture, and the context must be taken into consideration. The <u>context</u> includes the cultural background of the people who are being written or spoken to. The context also includes the particular situation the writer is addressing. Also to be considered is the "precedent," or the Law of First Mention, which gives us a pattern for interpretation. (See <u>Prove All Things Workbook</u>.)

In 1 Corinthians 14:34,35, where Paul said for women to "keep silence" in the churches, he was not talking to women in the ministry but women in a congregation who were out of order. Also, he was writing to the Corinthians, who were very carnal Christians and mostly Gentiles, so they had no background in customs of the synagogues. In fact, many of Paul's epistles dealt with local problems and his instructions are not meant to be taken as "commandments" across the board for all situations. On the other hand, we need to see what basic principle of God was involved in Paul's examples and instructions and follow that. For example, we have seen that his words about women's apparel have a basic principle of <u>modesty</u> for all generations. He did not give a commandment of not wearing makeup or pants suits, or women not cutting their hair.

Under the Old Covenant, there <u>was</u> separation between men and women, races, classes, and cultures. We see this from history and from Paul's comment that the "middle wall of partition" among mankind, or division by gender, class, or race, had been torn down in the New Covenant (Eph. 2:12-16). The tabernacle and temples segregated men and women. Therefore, many scholars believe that the Jewish Christians were disturbed by the outspokenness of the Gentile women in the early assemblies.

Charles Trombley of Tulsa, Oklahoma, a well-known evangelist and author, says in his book, Who Says Women Can't Teach?:

Dean Alford, an Anglican scholar during the nineteenth century said about Priscilla, a woman minister in the New Testament (1 Cor. 16:19), "Aquila (her husband) was a ready and zealous patron rather than a teacher. Priscilla had the gift, and her husband gave her support." W. H. Ramsay, who researched and wrote The Church in the Roman Empire, said, "In Asia Minor, women had equality with men. During this period Roman women were elevated to full and equal status without any distinction between the sexes."[2]

This was not true of Jewish nor Arabic women for centuries, although Christian women were accorded "full and equal" status in the Early Church. Even today, Arab and Palestinian women, along with some Asian women, do not have equality with the men. So in the early congregations where cultures were mixing as followers of Jesus, conflicts resulted which had to be resolved by an apostle.

Christ Unlimited — P.O. Box 850 — Dewey, AZ 86327   USA

Women Ministers in the Old and New Testaments

If we look at other things Paul wrote, we will see that he accepted women in the ministry, an entirely different subject than he was dealing with in the Corinthian epistles. Paul was addressing church order in 1 Corinthians 14:33-40, not women in ministry. In fact, because of Old Testament "precedents," apparently it never occurred to Paul or the early Christians to specifically address the subject of women in the ministry. They took it as a matter of course that Jesus would call and ordain anyone He chose — and that settled it!

As a matter of fact, the Bible mentions a prophetess who was in the temple when Jesus was brought there as a baby. Her name was Anna (Luke 2:36), and she was one of two people who recognized Jesus as the Messiah because of her sensitivity to the Holy Spirit. The other was Simeon (Luke 2:25-35). A man and a woman welcomed the Messiah, as well as the shepherds and the Wise Men at His birth. Some of the other things that Paul wrote showing he accepted women in the ministry include:

*Galatians 3:28, where the apostle said there is "neither male nor female" in the Body

*Romans 16:1,2, where Paul sent greetings to Phoebe, a "servant of the church at Cenchrea" and asked that the Christians at Rome not only receive her but help her in any way possible. Some believe she was a wealthy businesswoman, but from the term "a servant of the church," she sometimes was considered pastor, elder, or deacon.

*Romans 16:12, where he sent greetings to <u>Tryphena</u> and <u>Tryphosa</u>, who "labor in the Lord" and may have been "fellow deaconesses,"[3] also to Persis, whom he called "beloved." All were leaders of some sort in local churches. In the same chapter (v. 15), he mentioned Julia, along with male leaders whom he was greeting.

*1 Corinthians 16:19, where he sent his greetings to Aquila and Priscilla. Other references (Acts 18:2,3, 24-26) and early church writings tell us this couple pastored together, but "in three out of five places, her name appears first, evidence enough that she played the more important part in the early church. . . . Her prominence is evidenced by many facts. She became the teacher of the eloquent and learned Apollos. The church assembled in her home, both at Ephesus and at Rome, and she was known throughout Christendom in her day."[4]

*Romans 16:7 may be the most significant proof of women in the five-fold ministry in the early church. In that verse, Paul sent greetings to Andronicus and <u>Junia</u>, his "fellow-prisoners" who **are of note among the** <u>**apostles**</u>. <u>Junia</u> is a woman's name. In some modern translations, an "s" has been added (Junias) because the translators were so sure a woman could not be an apostle they thought a copyist had dropped the "s." However, the proper male ending would have been "ius," not "ias." No Church commentator earlier than the Middle Ages questioned that <u>Junia</u> was a woman and an apostle.[5]

Women played a major role in the ministry of Jesus. Some ask why He did not choose women disciples, if that is true. He could

Christ Unlimited — P.O. Box 850 — Dewey, AZ 86327   USA

not choose women among the 12 because women and men could not be traveling around the countryside together as singles. Also, the 12 disciples fulfilled the "type and shadow" of the twelve patriarchs, so they had to be equal to men (Rev. 21:12,14). But women were obviously accepted by Him as equals to men. (A good Bible study would be to find all of the women mentioned in the Gospels and see how Jesus acted toward them.)

In regard to women being prophetesses, we find many recorded in the Bible. Some think that in **Revelation 2:20**, Jesus pronounced judgment on a woman because she called herself "a prophetess." In those verses, He was not warning her because, as a woman, she had no right to be a prophetess. Instead, He warned of judgment because she "called herself," instead of His having called her. Also, she was leading the church into error.

For earlier precedents, we can look at the Old Testament history of Israel, which has types and shadows of things in the New Covenant. There we find women prophetesses — Miriam, sister of Moses, and Deborah, not only a prophetess but one of the judges of Israel. In addition to being a judge, she had a husband and went to war with an Israelite general (**Judg. 4,5; Heb. 11:32**). Also, there is Huldah (**2 Chron. 34:22-28**) who was consulted even before Jeremiah when the Book of the Law was found by King Josiah. And **Nehemiah 6:14** mentions Noadiah, "a prophetess." Examples of women who were prophetesses in the New Testament were Anna (**Luke 2:36-38**) and Phillip's daughters (**Acts 21:9**).

There are not as many women prophetesses, judges, and leaders in the Bible as men, nor are there as many called today.

However, we are not dealing with numbers but with <u>precedents</u> for the fact that women are used by God in leadership roles <u>as He chooses</u>.

Even today, the percentage of women in the ministry seems to be about the same as in the early Church. Of the four leading Pentecostal denominations, the percentage ranges from almost 4 to 15 percent with the Assembly of God having the most.[6] Adding in the major mainline churches, the percent has risen from 4 percent in 1977 to almost 8 percent by 1986.[7] However, numbers in the ministry should not be the goal or focus of Christian women but acceptance of <u>both</u> men and women by the Church as equally called of God to five-fold offices.

Since the Early Church, there have not been a lot of women spiritual leaders until the 20th century. In fact, not many women were ever in any kind of leadership positions over the ages — spiritually or otherwise. During the 1400s, Joan of Arc led France in her battles, and that was truly extraordinary. Most of the prejudice against women ministers today is not rooted in the Bible, but in the culture of the Middle Ages, when women truly were considered and treated as property. Only in the past 100 to 150 years have women been able to freely walk in the liberty restored to them by the redemptive work of the cross.

In the Wesleyan revival, women played prominent roles. By the mid 1700s, women were "prophesying" (preaching) in the Puritan movements, among the Quakers, and in other groups.[8] Within this century in the United States, we know of at least three major ministries led by women: Maria Woodworth-Etter, Aimee Semple

McPherson, and Kathryn Kuhlman. Also, an English woman, Jessie Penn-Lewis, was an important teacher and authoress at the turn of the century, who ministered in leadership during the Welsh Revival. We recommend all of her writings, which can be found at most Christian bookstores.[9]

One professor of church history wrote recently:

"The lives of women often provide the most faithful models of Christian discipleship. Ever since the day of the Resurrection, women have proclaimed the good news they discovered in Christit. . . . The prominence of women is conspicuous in every era of revival in the history of the church."[10]

Endnotes

[1]Hamon, Dr. Bill. <u>Prophets Pitfalls and Principles</u> (Shippensburg: Destiny Image, 1991), p. 107. His other books on this subject, published by the same firm, are <u>Prophets and the Prophetic Movement</u>, and <u>Prophets and Personal Prophecy</u>.

[2]Trombley, Charles. <u>Who Says Women Can't Teach?</u> (South Plainfield: Bridge Publishing Inc., 1985), p. 12.

[3]<u>Nelson's Illustrated Bible Dictionary</u> (Nashville: Thomas Nelson Publishers, 1986), p. 1076.

[4]Deen, Edith. <u>All of the Women of the Bible</u> (New York: Harper & Row, Publishers, 1955), p. 227-230. [Note: This is a good book to read for more Biblical and historical information on women's roles in the Old and New Testaments.]

[5]Giles, Kevin. <u>Patterns of Ministry Among the First Christians</u> (Melbourne: Collins Dove, 1989), pp. 166-168.

[6]Justice, Nancy. "Women Pastors Gain Acceptance," <u>Charisma & Christian Life</u> (Lake Mary: Strang Communications Co., July 1993, Vol. 18, No. 12), pp. 52,53.

[7]The Almanac of the Christian World, 1991-1992 edition, (Wheaton: Tyndale House Publishers, Inc., 1990), p. 377.

[8]Chilcote, Paul W. She Offered Them Christ (Nashville: Abingdon Press, 1993), pp. 12,13.

[9]Penn-Lewis, Jessie, War on the Saints and others, (Fort Washington, PA: The Christian Literature Crusade, abridged edition from the original British version). An unabridged edition is available from Thomas E. Lowe, Ltd., New York, ISBN #0-913926-03-5.

[10]Chilcote, p. 11.

Lesson for Section Two

[Author's Note: All Scripture references that answer these questions have been given. Please do not look at the answer pages until you have answered the questions in your own words. This is an expository lesson to help you learn.]

I. Jesus' Assignments to the Church

   A. Jesus gave the Church _____ in the form of men and women who were to lead the Church into perfection.

   Reference: Ephesians 4:4-16

   1. These "gifts" are called the _____ ministry offices. Name the offices:

      a. _____

      b. _____

      c. _____

      d. _____

      e. _____

2. They are to be called and _____ by Jesus.

3. They are chosen without regard to race, class, or _____.

Reference: Galatians 3:28

B. The purpose of the five-fold ministry gifts is to bring the entire Body of Christ into _____.
Reference: Ephesians 4:12,13

1. The chief office under Christ is the _____.

   a. Apostle comes from the Greek word meaning "_____," which is one requirement of an apostle as he is assigned a special task from the Lord.

   b. Other characteristics of the office of apostle include being anointed with special _____, _____, and _____.
   References: Acts 19:11; 2 Corinthians 12:12.

   c. Apostles are to help straighten out problems and _____ elders in local churches.
   References: Titus 1:5; Acts 14:23

d. Name some of the apostles listed in the New Testament:

_____

_____

_____

2. The second office is that of _____.

a. Prophets preach, but also speak forth _____
   at the unction of the Holy Spirit.

b. _____, as well as men, spoke the word of
   God forth prophetically in the Bible. Name some of the
   prophetesses in the Old and New Testaments:
   1) _____
   2) _____
   3) _____
   4) _____

3. The third office mentioned is that of _____.
   a. What is the assignment of the evangelist?

   _____.

   Reference: Mark 16:15-20

   b. Name two New Testament evangelists:
   _____ and _____

4. The fourth office is the most familiar to us today, and that is _____.

    a. What does the Greek word poimen, translated pastor, mean? _____
    Reference: 1 Peter 5:1,2

    b. What is the pastor's assignment?

    _____

    Reference: Acts 20:28

5. The fifth office, which has become very well-known in the past 20 years is that of _____.

    a. A teacher truly called and ordained of God will bring life to the Body by _____ teaching, not by intellectual teaching.

    b. The purpose of the teacher is to _____ and make clear the Word of God.
    References: Acts 1:1; 2 Timothy 2:2

C. Four types of church government, or order, have been developed during the past _____ years. Name three of them and give a brief description following the pattern of example:

Christ Unlimited — P.O. Box 850 — Dewey, AZ 86327   USA

1. Episcopal — rule by a bishop or other overseer

2. _____

3. _____

4. _____

II. The Role of Women in the Five-fold Ministry

A. Both _____ and _____ are included in the phrase, "sons of God."

1. Adam <u>and</u> Eve before the fall were originally created _____, and they were both named "Adam." Reference: Genesis 1:27, 5:2

2. Equality and true partnership were restored to men and women in the _____ Covenant through what Jesus did for all men and women on the cross. Reference: Romans 8:14-17

B. God makes no distinction between the sexes in the _____ of Christ.

Christ Unlimited — P.O. Box 850 — Dewey, AZ 86327   USA

There is one body, and one Spirit, even as ye are called in one hope of your calling; One Lord, one faith, one baptism.

Ephesians 4:4,5

1. Is it true that the Apostle Paul taught against women in the ministry? _____

2. What was he writing about to the Corinthians when he spoke of women keeping quiet in church services?

_____

3. When women preach or teach, are they "usurping authority over men?"

_____

   a. Whose authority do both men and women operate in within the five-fold offices? _____

   b. Name at least two New Testament women considered to have been pastors or deaconesses:

   _____ and _____

Christ Unlimited — P.O. Box 850 — Dewey, AZ 86327   USA

    c. Name the woman who seems to have held the office of
       apostle: _____

Overcoming Life Memory Verses

The suggested memory verses for this section are:

And he gave some, apostles; and some, prophets; and some, evangelists; and some, pastors and teachers; For the perfecting of the saints, for the work of the ministry, for the edifying of the body of Christ.

                                        Ephesians 4:21,22

There is neither Jew nor Greek, there is neither bond nor free, there is neither male nor female: for ye are all one in Christ Jesus. And if ye be Christ's, then are ye Abraham's seed, and heirs according to the promise.

                                        Galatians 3:28,29

Review Outline, Section Two

I. The Five-Fold Ministry Gifts

A. Both men and women are called into five-fold ministry offices.

   1. The New Testament shows many examples of women working in these offices, as well as in the offices of deaconess.

   2. The responsibility of these offices is to bring others into the maturity which they possess (Eph. 4:11-15).

B. The five-fold offices are apostle, prophet, evangelist, pastor and teacher.

   1. An apostle is "one sent forth" to establish the Kingdom life in the Church of Jesus Christ who are anointed with miracles, signs, and wonders.

   2. A prophet is one who preaches and expounds God's Word and, also, speaks divine utterances by the Holy Spirit.

   3. Evangelists are to take the gospel to the world in order to bring new converts into the Kingdom. They are also anointed to perform signs and wonders, miracles, and healings.

   4. Pastors are to lead and help the sheep to grow into the maturity of Christ.

   5. Teachers expound the Word of God to help others gain a better understanding of His ways and His will.

Christ Unlimited — P.O. Box 850 — Dewey, AZ 86327   USA

C. Women can serve in the five-fold ministry if qualified by God.

   1. Paul was not opposed to women teachers. (Rom. 16:1,2,12; 1 Cor. 14:31)

   2. 1 Corinthians 14:34,35 deals with a problem of disorder in the Corinthian Church not with general rules for the Church at large through all generations.

   3. Women can teach men as long as they are in submission to the Headship of Jesus and under the unction of the Holy Spirit (Acts 18:24-26).

   4. 1 Timothy 2:11-15 refers to wives who have not yet learned to be submissive in the home.

II. Women Ministers in the Old and New Testament

   A. Old Testament Examples

      1. Deborah, the judge and prophetess (Judg. 4,5)

      2. Huldah, a prophetess in King Josiah's time (2 Chron. 34:22-28)

   B. New Testament examples before the New Covenant

      1. Anna, a prophetess in the Temple when Jesus was brought there as a baby (Luke 2:36,37).

      2. Mary and Elizabeth, who both prophesied, although they were not known as prophetesses (Luke 1).

   C. New Testament examples after the New Covenant

      1. Phoebe of Cenchrea (Rom. 16:1)

      2. Tryphena and Persis (Rom. 16:12)

      3. Priscilla (Acts 18:2,3, 24-26)

      4. Junia (Rom. 16:7)

III. Women in the Ministry Today

A. In spite of God calling more and more women into the ministry today, there is still great resistance to them by some.

B. In Pentecostal-Charismatic denominations, women range from 3 to 15 percent of the ministers.

C. The Church should not be trying to get more women into the ministry (that is God's business) but trying to get those God ordains accepted without prejudice.

Review Outline Quiz, Section Two

1. Can women hold five-fold ministry offices? _____

2. Was Paul opposed to women teachers? _____

3.   How do we know this from the Bible?

    _____

4. What was Paul addressing in his letter to the Corinthians, when he discussed women speaking publicly?

    _____

5. Were there women leaders of Israel in Old Testament days?

    _____

6. Name a woman judge: _____

7. Did Paul include women in his thanks and appreciation to his fellow laborers in the Lord? _____

8. Who is the most well-known female teacher and church leader in the New Testament? _____

9. Are women generally accepted today in the ministry?

    _____

10. Which Pentecostal-Charismatic denomination has the largest percentage of women in ministry? _____

Neither Male Nor Female Workbook

Section Three

"The Biblical Pattern of Wholeness for Women"

Christ Unlimited — P.O. Box 850 — Dewey, AZ 86327   USA

Neither Male Nor Female Workbook
Section Three: "The Biblical Pattern of Wholeness for Women"
Expository Introduction

God is using more and more women in the ministry in these closing hours of the Church even as He did in Paul's day, during the beginning of the Church. Philippians 4:3 could have been addressed to men in the ministry today just as Paul entreated his fellow ministers in that day:

And I entreat thee also, true yoke-fellow, help those women which laboured with me in the gospel, with Clement also, and with other my fellow-labourers, whose names are in the book of life.

In the early Church, as we saw in the last Section, and up until about A.D. 500, women ministered along with men. Church history, particularly records of various church councils during those years, reveals that bishops were charged to ordain women deaconesses. These women taught, ministered, and were called "clerics." However, by the year A.D. 532, the Council of Orleans ruled in error against women ministering:

The leaders of the Church "took it all the way back to the traditions of Jewish elders: 'No longer shall the blessing of women deaconnesses be given, because of the weakness of the sex.' ...By this time in church history, the doctrinal, moral, and spiritual apostasy was nearly complete, and many practices of the church were foreign to the Scripture."[1]

Not allowing women to minister in the Church dates from the Middle Ages' perversion of the Church becoming an institution instead of being a family as God originally ordained. Many wonderful truths have been restored since the Reformation, but the truth of women in ministry being accepted is just now beginning to be restored as Biblical and God-ordained. Although in many churches, women are accepted in ministries, they still face various problems. One stems from those men and women who still believe that women cannot hold a five-fold ministry office. Two other concerns are whether or not women should have a "male covering" and the kinds of fashions they wear in clothes, hair, and make-up.

The "male-covering" doctrine was developed over the last two centuries to satisfy the prejudice against women ministers, yet not totally forbid women to preach. This "qualification" or condition for women to preach was that those who did take the pulpit must have "male coverings" over them. The "male (or head) covering," was defined as no woman to preach or teach without some male minister's approval and his authority over her, which was her "covering." The basis for this was an interpretation of 1 Corinthians 11:3-16 which was made without knowledge of the cultural customs of Paul's day that he was really addressing.

In those verses, Paul instructed men not to come into the local meetings with their heads covered and women not to come without their heads being covered. The early church meetings were held in homes or in rented public halls. There were no "church buildings" as we know them today. It is necessary to know the history of "head coverings" to truly understand Paul's words.

The Facts Behind "Head Coverings"

Paul wrote every woman that prayeth or prophesieth (v. 4); so, Paul obviously had no problem with women being used by God to pray or prophesy in public. The clash in Corinth between Jewish Christians — whose women were accustomed to being veiled, to being completely silent in public, and even totally separated from the men in synagogues — and Gentile women who had different customs created a conflict in the local bodies. That is the situation behind Paul's words to the Corinthians about head coverings.

Without a head covering, it would have been hard to survive in the hot desert sun so much closer to the equator than we are in America. The men and women of Saudi Arabia, Kuwait, and other Arabic nations still wear full robes and head coverings, much as the Israelites and Jews did in Bible days.

Jewish men today still wear a yarmulke (a skullcap) as a token covering on their heads in synagogues and certain other situations. However, Paul wrote that Christ was now the covering of men, so they should not go into services with head coverings as if Christ had not come (1 Cor. 11:3,4). Today, both men and women who are born again have the "helmet of salvation" covering their heads (Eph. 6:17).

Nevertheless (or "on the other hand") neither is the man without the woman, neither is the woman without the man, in the Lord.

1 Corinthians 11:11

That means men and women are not independent of one another, because the first woman came from man, but all men since then come from women (1 Cor. 11:12). And, <u>both</u> men and women originated with God, so in the final analysis, Jesus is now the spiritual covering (our helmet of salvation) for all of God's children.

Some men have used 1 Corinthians 11:3 as justification for the "male covering" doctrine.

But I would have you know, that the head of every man is Christ; and the head of the woman is the man; and the head of Christ is God.

They interpret that verse to mean that every man is the head of every woman, so unless a woman is married or ministering within a church under a male pastor, she can not preach. Kenneth E. Hagin wrote:

Our text (1 Cor. 11:3) cannot mean that <u>every</u> man stands in the same relationship to every woman as Christ does to every man. That could not be true... If that were the case women could never be saved unless their husbands told them they could... Christ is the head of the woman just as much as He is the head of the man. If

He isn't — then the woman is not in the church, for Christ is the head of the Church.[2]

Also it would mean any man could tell any woman what to do. Actually, in Paul's writings, we are dealing with three things concerning women:

1. A woman's spiritual head is Christ.
2. A woman's head in marriage is her husband.
3. A woman's physical covering is her hair, which is <u>symbolic</u> of the intangible coverings of her husband and of Jesus.

Old Testament customs were that women seldom cut their hair, and some had hair long enough to sit on, or longer. And when Paul talked about long hair being a disgrace to men, he meant as long as women's hair was then (1 Cor. 11:14). Men wore their hair probably about shoulder-length. The short men's haircuts of today originated in World War I as a preventive against head lice in the armed services. In portraits of Civil War days, for example, most of the men had hair shoulder-length also.

Customs Are Not Biblical Commands

In other words, Paul was saying (1 Cor. 11:16) that how men or women wear their hair is a matter of tradition or custom. Today, we would say it is a matter of "fashion." The principle underlying Paul's writings on the appearance of women is <u>modesty</u> (1 Tim. 2:9,10). Modesty is the same in any society and culture: Not dressing to draw attention to oneself and not displaying more flesh than is decent.

In fact, in Bible days, women apparently did cut their hair at times. One of the vows of a Nazarite, a person separated unto God for a certain period of time, meant that a man or a woman would not cut their hair (Num. 6:2-8). So, if women never cut their hair, there would have been no reason for them to vow not to in this case.

Concerning clothes, Paul said women should not wear men's clothes, nor men women's. Again, he was not talking about women's pants suits or jeans, nor was he talking about men wearing bathrobes. He was talking about transvestitism, or "cross-dressing," which is very prevalent in the homosexual and lesbian communities.

Actually, both Jewish men and women in Paul's day wore what we would consider "dresses." They wore robes of a certain length with cloaks or outer robes over them. Pants for men are a fairly recent fashion. In the Middle Ages, men wore tights with short tops, and this lasted until into the 18th century. Even then, men's pants were fitted to the legs like leggings. One of the marks of a handsome man of George Washington's day was "a well-turned leg."

So Paul could not have been talking about robe-style dresses opposed to pants. He and all of his day would probably have been shocked to see the way men dress today, as much so as to see modern women's styles!

A woman who ministers in foreign countries should be courteous enough to find out the customs for women's dress there

Christ Unlimited — P.O. Box 850 — Dewey, AZ 86327   USA

and follow them. She does not have to wear native dress, but if the custom is for women not to expose their shoulders and arms, for example, then she should wear long sleeves and higher necks. A woman missionary in Arab lands who wore very short skirts would bring shame on the Lord's message in their eyes. This would defeat her purpose in ministry. But this is not done to follow a commandment of God, it is simply to "be all things to all people," as Paul said (1 Cor. 9:20-23).

The true covering of God over any man or woman has nothing to do with outward styles. It is rather a spiritual covering (Isa. 30:1). Even God has a "covering." It is His glory, or His light. He is "clothed with honor and majesty" (Ps. 104:1,2). Satan first came into being as God's "anointed cherub that covereth" (Ezek. 28:14). He is thought to have been the most beautiful creature ever created by God, because he was a cherub designed to cover the throne. He was an angelic order of being, but not an angel as we generally think of angels. He was of a higher order of being.

A woman's matrimonial head, or covering, is her husband, but her spiritual Head is Christ (1 Cor. 11:3). Therefore, we can see that a single woman can minister without being under the headship of a natural man. She is under the headship of Jesus.

On the other hand, a wife who is disrespectful of her husband and who has usurped the authority of headship certainly should not be in the pulpit. If anyone, man or woman, is not able to submit to earthly authority, that person will not submit to the Holy Spirit. There have been a few women who have even left their husbands and children to "go minister for God," which certainly was <u>not</u> God. A woman ministering out of spiritual order is the same as having her head shaved (1 Cor. 11:6); in other words, she is bringing shame on the Lord.

According to the Bible, husbands and wives should cover one another with love and prayers (1 Pet. 3:7-12). If a wife does something to dishonor or embarrass her husband, she is left "naked" because they are one flesh (Gen. 2:24; Mark 10:6-9). If she has despised (been contemptuous of) her husband in any way, she has uncovered <u>him</u>. King David's wife Michal, Saul's daughter, despised her husband, and it caused the curse of barrenness to come upon her as she had no children (2 Sam. 6:20-23). As a spiritual principle, a woman who has despised her husband cannot do a real work for God. She could birth no spiritual children.

On the other hand, a husband who will not fill the role of high priest in his home, and who does not love and cherish his wife is not covering her in the way that he ought (Eph. 5:25,28-33).

Husbands and wives can have powerful ministries together, if they will submit to God and to each other (1 Pet. 3:7-12). Ideally, a man and woman should first learn to love one another as a brother and sister in the Lord before marrying. As they respect one another in this way, God can use them as a ministry team. God has blessed us personally with such a ministry, and it is very rewarding. However, some people even criticize women with this type of ministry. In some areas of the Church today, even women ministering with their husbands run into problems. Dr. Bill Hamon writes:

"Not long ago, for example, we ran into a problem when we discovered that a group that had invited me to minister did not believe in women ministers. My wife nearly always travels with me in ministry as a co-speaker and prophetic minister; she and I come as a "package deal," and for years our hosts have willingly paid travel expenses for both of us. So I insisted that she be with me on this trip as well. But our hosts refused to pay for my wife's ticket, which was over six hundred dollars."[3]

Dr. Hamon explained that although they had to personally pay for his wife's ticket and received the lowest offering in a decade for four days of ministry, the Lord made it up to them the following week with an exceptionally large offering at another four-day meeting. So, if both husband and wife are in God's will and have their motives and attitudes right before Him, He will take care of their needs in spite of people's wrong reactions toward them.

Jesus' Words Concerning Marriage and Divorce

In the Gospels, Jesus is recorded as answering questions from various scribes and Pharisees concerning marriage. In His day, polygamy was still practiced in places, and divorce was even easier than today — at least for men. But women had no right to divorce their husbands for any reason. This situation is what Jesus was addressing in Matthew 19:3-9.

In those verses, Jesus was saying, "My Father's design was for there to be one man and one woman faithful to one another and

Christ Unlimited — P.O. Box 850 — Dewey, AZ 86327   USA

joined in one flesh. It is not lawful for a man to put his wife away for just any cause. Moses' provision for divorce was because men had hardened hearts (insensitive to God and to others). Moses had to instruct men that, if they were going to put away their wives, <u>they at least had to give them a legal paper</u> for the wives' sakes. However, if a divorce occurs for any reason but fornication on the part of one of the parties, it is sin."

Paraphrasing, His disciples said, "Well, if we cannot get rid of wives who do not please us the way our fathers have always done, we would be better off not to marry at all (v. 10)!"

Jesus said that under the New Covenant stricter morality is required (Matt. 5:27-32). It is not only a sin to physically commit adultery, but lusting in one's heart after someone of the opposite sex is the <u>same</u> as committing adultery. Also, by His statements on marriage and divorce, Jesus abolished polygamy, which was still practiced by Jews in some instances. Jesus was directly correcting the men to whom He spoke in these passages, not women.

Actually, He spoke of an unprecedented possibility for women. In Mark 10:12, Jesus said, "And if she herself divorces her husband . . . ." Until His day, women never divorced their husbands in Israel or Judah. It was not allowed. How could a "possession" divorce its owner? The woman at the well (John 4:6-42) had five husbands (v. 18) — but she was a Samaritan, not a Jew.

Even today in the modern nation of Israel, many customs are the same as in Judah during Jesus' day. Divorce, marital, and family matters come under religious courts, not civil. Men can divorce their wives the same as in ancient times (by appearing before a panel of three rabbis) and remarry, but unless a husband gives his wife a "bill of divorcement," she cannot remarry.[4]

Since the time of Ezra, the rabbis, scribes, and Pharisees had perverted the Mosaic Law into "The Law," a much more legalistic and bondage-making set of rules and regulations than the Mosaic law around which this oral tradition was built. This is what Jesus called "the doctrines and traditions of men" (Matt. 15:3-9; Mark 7:6-13) that made the will and Word of God of no avail. Out of this overemphasis on legalism after the Babylonian exile came the Jewish attitudes that women were the cause of all sin and were the property of men just as their oxen or their donkeys. Women had no rights in Jewish society of Jesus' day. Their status had steadily declined in Judah since the exile.

... Women were considered chattels along with slaves, houses, land, and animals... A woman had no recourse even if a man infected her with venereal disease or inflicted brutality on her. The rabbis, however, would have argued that they had a scriptural basis for their halacha (ruling). The tenth commandment says: **Thou shalt not covet thy neighbour's wife ...nor his ass.** From that statement the rabbis concluded that wives were classified with animals and other property... That is why they brought the woman (taken in adultery) but not the man to Jesus for His judgment, and that's why He reacted violently to their hypocrisy... Only men spoke in public. No woman could give a testimony or conduct business. Generally, the attitude toward women was one of disregard, subjugation, and repression... Women, children, slaves, and imbeciles are linked together (in the Mishnah and Talmud) and exempted from knowing or fulfilling the law since they were all subordinate to their masters.[5]

From reading the history of cultural and social customs in Bible times and from understanding the difference between what the New Testament Jews meant by the law and what Jesus meant by the law, we can see that both Jesus _and_ Paul were not prejudiced against women. Actually, both were being revolutionary in lifting women back to the position to which God created them to occupy. This brings new understanding to Paul's words that after the New Covenant there are no more differences between gender, race, social class, etc. (Gal. 3:28).

The court of the women (in the Temple) was free of buildings and surrounded with a gallery so that the women should not mingle with the men....Separation was the premise on which the Temple was constructed, making a clear distinction between man and God, Jew and Gentile, male and female, priest and people. Archeological research and data bear out this distinction: the remains of ancient synagogues in Galilee show the galleries, although some scholars deny that these were for women since women were excluded from any active role in public worship. One fact emerges: Jewish women never asked their husbands questions in public. In the Temple, they did not sit opposite them; they were segregated some fifteen steps below them. They were silenced "as also saith the Law."[6]

Paul's Advice on Marriage and Divorce

Paul's advice was for a man or a woman who became Christian to stay with the unsaved partner, if that person would allow it. However, he felt it was better for anyone in the Lord's work to remain single, but he said that was <u>his</u> advice, not God's (1 Cor. 7:7,8,32-40), because he said "after <u>my</u> judgment" (v. 40). His reasoning was that a single woman could focus her entire attention on Jesus and His work, whereas a married woman had to first please and look after her husband. And the same is true of men.

Paul took his own advice and never married; however, Peter and many of the other apostles had wives. And, as we saw in the earlier sections, many women who played major roles in the early Church also were married. Celibacy and marriage are equally acceptable to God, as long as He is first in either case (Luke 14:26,33). Love for God should come before love for one's husband or wife, children, or parents. God must be number one in all of our lives.

Love is not an emotion, but a choice and a commitment. Even in a marriage that has problems, if the one who is saved will <u>choose</u> to love God first and the spouse by choice, God can work in that marriage.

Emotion is what we feel that expresses or reflects love. It is not love itself. Genuine love is defined by Paul in 1 Corinthians 13. He defined it by what love <u>does</u>, not by what love <u>feels</u>.

Single men and women who choose marriage are not to marry unbelievers, Paul said. Being unequally yoked with an unbeliever is simply asking for trouble (2 Cor. 6:14,15).

Paul's instructions that elders of churches be **the husband of one wife** simply meant that, in a polygamous society, Christians should not have concubines or several wives at the same time (1 Tim. 3:2). These guidelines were given so that no reproach would be brought upon Jesus or His Church in the eyes of the world.

Guidelines included having one's homelife in order (marriage and children), not acting like sinners, and not putting those who were novices in leadership positions. New Christians may get into pride if they are given high offices before attaining some spiritual maturity (1 Tim. 3:1-6; 1 Pet. 3:1-8).

How does God deal with the sin of divorce?

Unbelievers come to God repenting for <u>all sins</u> in one package; believers come to God repenting for each specific sin of omission and commission. These sins are already under the blood, but for the sake of maintaining a pure conscience, they must be dealt with. Also, any unconfessed sin gives the devil a foothold in a Christian's life.

Of course, any sin that occurred before a person is "born again" is totally wiped out in God's eyes as if it had never occurred. Divorce before conversion means a person can remarry without any qualms. In God's eyes, that earlier marriage never occurred.

Christ Unlimited — P.O. Box 850 — Dewey, AZ 86327   USA

Unsaved people are not joined by God, although they are legally bound. However, if one becomes a Christian while married, he is to remain in that marriage even if the mate does not confess Jesus at the same time (1 Cor. 7:27). God desires to use the believer to convert the unbeliever.

If, however, the unbeliever hardens his or her heart and desires to depart from the marriage, the believer is to let them go if the unbeliever insists on dissolving the marriage. The believer then is no longer under any bondage and is free to marry again as the Lord leads (1 Cor. 7:12-16,39).

God is against divorce. He hates the "putting away" of mates (Mal. 2:14-16). God does not condone broken vows and division. However, if divorce occurs, it is not the unpardonable sin, even for Christians.

No sin is big enough to cost us salvation except that of crucifying Christ anew and blaspheming the Holy Spirit (Matt. 12:31,32; Heb. 6:4-8). However, we must confess our sins and be forgiven (1 John 1:9). Divorce should be repented of as any other sin and placed under the blood of Jesus.

God can erase the sin of divorce as much as any other sin. If a divorced person seeks forgiveness for divorce as sin, that person can remarry (Heb. 10:17). However, Christians who blithely divorce thinking God is always forgiving and permissive will run into trouble. A person who commits sin, premeditating that God will forgive him, is not really repentive and will reap what he is sowing.

The Greek word for repentance means to completely turn around and go the other way. Those who claim to be saved and keep marrying and getting divorced are misusing the grace of God. They are using God's mercy as a license to sin and, in the process, trampling on the blood of Jesus.

The Bible's Ideal Woman

Women with young children would be able to be better wives and mothers if they remained at home with their love, strength, and energy being devoted to the family, even as Scripture outlines.

The aged women likewise, that they be in behavior as becometh holiness, not false accusers, not given to much wine, teachers of good things. That they may teach the young women to be sober, to love their husbands, to love their children, To be discreet, chaste, keepers at home, good, obedient to their own husbands, that the Word of God be not blasphemed.

Titus 2:3-5

The question of whether women should work outside the home is not as controversial as it was a couple of decades ago. Now more women work than do not. In today's economy, most of those who work do so out of necessity. They are either single parents, or it takes two salaries for a family to make ends meet. The Lord gives grace and mercy when this is the case. However, when women use outside work as an escape from their domestic duties, this is

Christ Unlimited — P.O. Box 850 — Dewey, AZ 86327   USA

sin. Other motives such as competition with their husbands' abilities, lust for material things, and so forth are also sinful.

The Bible gives an example of an ideal woman as depicted in the scriptures and is found in Proverbs 31:10-31:

*She worked and made money, although she did it from her home.

*She also kept her home in perfect order.

*She brought credit and honor to her husband in the community.

*She brought up her children properly. Children should be trained early in the ways of the Lord (Prov. 22:6, 29:15).

*She was virtuous.

*She was a good administrator, having a staff of servants to disperse the different tasks.

*She was thrifty and farsighted, making certain supplies were laid in and clothing ready for the cold months.

*She spoke with wisdom and kindness.

*She was not lazy.

Women who minister and who are able to maintain their homes and take care of their families certainly may do so with God's blessing. However, if a woman has small children and no help at home, it would be better for her to stay home and properly nurture her children in the ways of the Lord. Many women are neglecting their husbands, homes, and children, as already mentioned, simply because they desire to escape domestic responsibility to pursue a "more exciting" life in the working world.

God judges us on our motives, and if we are uncaring in regard to our families, we are in sin, as are women who work outside the home with the wrong motives. However, God's grace will be with any Christian woman who is forced to make a living for her family. Many single mothers are in this position, and if they ask God to be their "husbands" and a Father to their children, He certainly will fill in the void. The Lord is there to help women with any problems they have, whether in their homes or their ministries.

We pray this workbook has cleared up any confusion in students' minds as to a woman's place at home and in the ministry.

Christ Unlimited — P.O. Box 850 — Dewey, AZ 86327   USA

Endnotes

[1]Trombley, <u>Who Says Women Can't Teach?</u>, p. 197.

[2]Hagin, Kenneth E. <u>The Woman Question</u> (Greensburg: Manna Christian Outreach, 1975), p. 20,21.

[3]Hamon, <u>Prophets Pitfalls and Principles</u>, pp. 92,93.

[4]Trombley, pp. 38,39.

[5]Ibid, pp. 31,32; Wight, Fred, <u>Manners and Customs of Bible Lands</u> (Chicago: Moody Press, 1953), p. 125.

[6]Trombley, p. 35.

Christ Unlimited — P.O. Box 850 — Dewey, AZ 86327   USA

Lesson for Section Three

I. Women's Problems in the Home and Ministry

A. Women and "Male Covering"

1. Women being veiled in New Testament times was only a

_____,

according to Paul's conclusion.
Reference: 1 Corinthians 11:3-16

But if any man seem to be contentious, we have no such custom, neither the churches of God.

1 Corinthians 11:16

2. A woman's physical covering is her _____.

But if a woman have long hair, it is a glory to her: for her hair is given her for a covering.

1 Corinthians 11:15

a. A born again woman's matrimonial head is her _____

_____.

Reference: Ephesians 5:23

b. A woman's spiritual head is _____.
Reference: Galatians 3:26-28

Christ Unlimited — P.O. Box 850 — Dewey, AZ 86327   USA

3. God's covering over any man or woman is not a physical one of veils and hats, but rather a _____ one.

Woe to the rebellious children, saith the Lord, that take counsel, but not of me; and that cover with a covering, but not of my spirit, that they may add sin to sin.

Isaiah 30:1

Bless the Lord, O my soul. O Lord my God, thou art very great; thou art clothed with honour and majesty. Who coverest thyself with light as with a garment: who stretchest out the heavens like a curtain.

Psalm 104:1,2

4. Man's Head also is _____.
   Reference: 1 Corinthians 11:3

   a. Covering one's head in the Old Testament was a sign of grief or _____ before God.
      References: Esther 6:12
                  2 Sam. 1:2

   b. After Christ came and ratified the New Covenant, it was the opposite from Old Covenant days and was considered _____ for men to <u>cover</u> their heads before God.

Every man praying or prophesying, having his head covered, dishonoureth his head.

1 Corinthians 11:4

    c.   For a born again man to cover his head before God would mean he would cover his _____.

Ye are the light of the world. A city that is set on an hill cannot be hid. Neither do men light a candle, and put it under a bushel, but on a candlestick; and it giveth light unto all that are in the house. Let your light so shine before men, that they may see your good works, and glorify your Father which is in heaven.

Matthew 5:14-16

5. Husbands and wives are to _____ one another.
    Reference: 1 Corinthians 11:11,12

    a.   One way women can cover their husbands is by the pure words of their _____.
       Reference: Ephesians 4:29
             James 3:2-13

    b.   Other ways husbands and wives can cover one another are by love and _____.
       Reference: Ephesians 6:18
             1 Pet. 3:1-12

II. Paul's Advice to Women About Marriage

A. Paul thought it was better for both men and women ministers to remain _____.
   Reference: 1 Corinthians 7:7,8,32-40

   1. Paul made it clear, however, that this was only his _____, not a command from God.
      Reference: 1 Corinthians 7:40

   2. God blesses both celibacy and marriage in His service, as long as _____.
      References: Luke 14:26,33 Hebrews 13:4

   But and if thou marry, thou hast not sinned... .

                                        1 Corinthians 7:28

      a. Love is not a feeling, but a _____ and a

         _____.

         Reference: 1 Corinthians 13

He that hath my commandments and keepeth them, he it is that loveth me: and he that loveth me shall be loved of my Father, and I will love him, and will manifest myself to him.

                                        John 14:21

Christ Unlimited — P.O. Box 850 — Dewey, AZ 86327   USA

b. Those who are not married but choose to get married are admonished to seek a _____ in order not to be unequally yoked.
Reference: **2 Corinthians 6:14**

c. Therefore, marriage for a Christian should be based only on direction from the _____.

B. If a man or woman gets saved, it is God's directive for that person to remain with the unsaved partner in order that the unbelieving one be _____.
Reference: **1 Corinthians 7:10-16**

1. If the unbelieving spouse insists on leaving, Paul said to let that person _____.
Reference: **1 Corinthians 7:13-15**

2. Husbands and wives should consider their _____ as belonging to one another.
Reference: **1 Corinthians 7:2-4**

a. The only time husbands or wives are to withhold sex from one another is:

_____

b. Also, both should be in _____ on this abstinence.

c. Paul's reason why husbands and wives should not withhold sex from one another and should consider their bodies as belonging to the other one was so that _____.

Reference for a, b, and c: 1 Corinthians 7:5

C. The first thing that needs to be confessed to God about divorce is that it is _____.

1. God hates _____, but not divorcees.
   Reference: Malachi 2:14-16

2. Divorces before being born again are covered by Jesus' blood, just as are other sins. To God, those past sins are _____.

And their sins and iniquities will I remember no more.
                                                    Hebrews 10:17

3. Divorce and remarriage for Christians should be _____ of as broken vows and adultery.
   Reference: Matthew 5:31,32

a. Can Christians be forgiven for divorce and remarriage?
   _____

References: 1 John 1:9; Hebrews 10:17

Christ Unlimited — P.O. Box 850 — Dewey, AZ 86327   USA

b. If this is repented of, but then repeated, it is
_____, sin that invites destruction in one's life.
Reference: 1 Cor. 10:8,9

For, brethren, ye have been called unto liberty, only use not
liberty for an occasion to the flesh, but by love serve one
another.

Galatians 5:13

4. When Paul wrote that a bishop should be the "husband
of one wife," did he mean a church leader could not be
divorced and remarried? _____
Reference: 1 Timothy 3:2

1. What did he mean, in the social context of the times?

_____

_____

2. Another thing Paul dealt with concerning wives of
leaders or women in ministry was their _____
_____.

In like manner also, that women adorn themselves in
modest apparel . . . .

1 Timothy 2:9

III. The Ideal Woman in Scripture: Proverbs 31:10-31

Who can find a virtuous woman? for her price is far above rubies. The heart of her husband doth safely trust in her, so that he shall have no need of spoil. She will do him good and not evil all the days of her life. She seeketh wool, and flax, and worketh willingly with her hands. She is like the merchants' ships: she bringeth her food from afar. She riseth also while it is yet night, and giveth meat to her household, and a portion to her maidens. She considereth a field, and buyeth it: with the fruit of her hands she planteth a vineyard. She girdeth her loins with strength, and strengtheneth her arms. She perceiveth that her merchandise is good: her candle goeth not out by night. She layeth her hands to the spindle, and her hands hold the distaff. She stretcheth out her hand to the poor; yea, she reacheth forth her hands to the needy. She is not afraid of the snow for her household: for all her household are clothed with scarlet. She maketh herself coverings of tapestry; her clothing is silk and purple. Her husband is known in the gates, when he sitteth among the elders of the land. She maketh fine linen, and selleth it; and delivereth girdles unto the merchant. Strength and honour are her clothing; and she shall rejoice in time to come. She openeth her mouth with wisdom; and in her tongue is the law of kindness. She looketh well to the ways of her household, and eateth not the bread of idleness. Her children arise up, and

Christ Unlimited — P.O. Box 850 — Dewey, AZ 86327   USA

call her blessed; her husband also, and he praiseth her. Many daughters have done virtuously, but thou excellest them all. Favour is deceitful, and beauty is vain: but a woman that feareth the Lord, she shall be praised. Give her of the fruit of her hands; and let her own works praise her in the gates.

A. According to these guidelines, may a woman work for money as well as keep house? _____
Reference: Proverbs 31:24

   1. Today, "making fine linen and selling it" is the equivalent of working _____.

   2. What is the main thing in these verses that brings a virtuous woman praise?

    _____

   3. She will be praised by _____.
Reference: Proverbs 31:28

B. Particularly in the New Testament, people are used by God on the basis of God's calling and their _____ to that calling, not on the basis of gender.

There is neither Jew nor Greek, there is neither bond nor free, there is neither male nor female: for ye are all one in Christ Jesus.

                                        Galatians 3:28

C. What did Paul ask his fellowmen in ministry to do concerning women in the ministry? _____.

And I entreat thee also, true yoke-fellow, help those women which laboured with me in the gospel . . . .

                                        Philippians 4:3

Overcoming Life Memory Verses

The suggested memory verses for this section are:

The "Love" or "Charity" chapter in the Bible. (Look it up.)

1 Corinthians 13

Be ye not unequally yoked together with unbelievers: for what fellowship hath righteousness with unrighteousness? and what communion hath light with darkness?

2 Corinthians 6:14

Christ Unlimited — P.O. Box 850 — Dewey, AZ 86327   USA

Review Outline, Section Three

I. Women's Problems in the Home and Ministry

   A. Erroneous beliefs about women in ministry dating from about A.D. 500 include:

   1. Women cannot minister at all. (However, Scripture declares otherwise, as indicated below.)

      a. In Jesus, there is neither male nor female (Gal. 3:28).

      b. Jesus had many women disciples while He was on earth (Luke 8:1-3; Matt. 27:55; Acts 1:14,15).

   2. Women must be under male headship to minister. (This too is an unscriptural view.)

      a. Old Testament women, such as Deborah, were not under male headship. She was judge over Israel, the highest national office in her day (Judg. 4).

      b. New Testament women mentioned by Paul were not all under a husband or male head.

   3. Women must have their heads physically covered when ministering.

      a. Again, this is a tradition from the Middle-Ages Church that became known to us as Roman Catholic.

      b. Covering the head was a Jewish custom, not a church ordinance (1 Cor. 11:16).

      c. Paul was opposed to imposing Jewish legalism on converts to Christianity (Acts 15:1-31).

B. The facts about "coverings" are:

  1. True covering is spiritual, not physical (Isa. 30:1; Ps. 104:1,2).

    a. Believers are covered with the helmet of salvation, or in other words, by Jesus through the Holy Spirit.

    b. In ministry, whether married or single, a woman's Head is Jesus, the same as a man's.

  2. A woman's head in marriage is her husband.

    a. Husbands and wives are to prefer one another, walking in mutual covering. He covers her by loving her as Christ loves the Church, and she covers him by respecting and honoring him.

    b. Both "cover" one another by not exposing any faults to outsiders.

    c. All Christians are to cover one another's sins with mercy and compassion.

  3. A woman should not seek a ministry at the expense of her husband and family.

II. Paul's Advice About Marriage

  A. Marriage is God's original plan for men and women (Heb. 13:4; 1 Tim. 3:1-7; Titus 1:5-10).

    1. Celibacy is acceptable for some believers (1 Cor. 7:8,9).

    2. Those seeking a mate should let God provide, not self.

    3. Marriage should be based on God's love, not emotion (1 Cor. 13).

4. The decision to marry should be directed by the Holy Spirit.

5. Believers should only marry other believers. (2 Cor. 6:14).

B. Divorce is sin.

1. Except on grounds of fornication, divorce can cause one or both parties to commit adultery (Matt. 5:31,32).

2. But divorce is not the unpardonable sin (John 8:4-11).

3. Christians should not judge one another over previous divorces, but extend mercy (James. 2:10-13).

4. God, in His grace, has made provision for forgiveness of divorce and remarriage.

a. Believers may divorce and remarry if the unbelieving partner wishes to depart (1 Cor. 7:13-15).

b. Believers who divorce and remarry out of the will of God may be forgiven and can still serve God in the ministry if they are truly repentant.

c. Divorce should never be used to take advantage of God's grace or just to escape an unpleasant situation.

III. Keys to a Happy Home and Family

A. How a wife can balance household responsibilities with spiritual pursuits:

1. Take the woman portrayed in Proverbs 31:10-31 as an example.

      a. A woman's primary responsibility is to her home and family (Titus 2:4,5).

      b. However, God must come first in her life.

   2. On the other hand, Christian women should be careful to avoid being like Martha (Luke 10:38-42).

      a. Martha placed natural things above the spiritual.

      b. Her sister, Mary, concentrated on Jesus.

B. The first step is to learn submission, a necessary ingredient for a compatible union (1 Cor. 11:3; Eph. 5:21-25).

   1. Unsubmissiveness, female domination, or a Jezebel spirit can ruin a home (Isa. 3:12).

   2. Extreme submission (being a doormat with no strength of spirit) is not God's will either.

   3. Anger, contention, and resentment must be repented of before a woman can be the wife and mother God intended (Prov. 21:19).

C. Older women are to teach the younger how to honor, love, and respect their husbands (Titus 2:3-5).

   1. The Lord, their Maker, will be the "husband" of widows (Isa. 54:5).

   2. Older women can serve in the ministry also. Since the Day of Pentecost, the Holy Spirit has been poured out upon all flesh, God's "sons and daughters" (Acts 2:17,18).

D. How women should dress, according to Scripture:

   1. A woman should dress modestly with real beauty coming

from within, not attracting attention to the body or to self (1 Tim. 2:9,10).

2. Just as in Proverbs 31, a woman should "adorn" herself with good works and the virtue of the Lord.

Review Outline Quiz, Section Three

1. List three erroneous beliefs about women being in ministry:

   a. _____

   b. _____

   c. _____

2. True coverings for men and women are _____ not physical.

3. How do husbands and wives "cover" one another?

   _____

4. Is divorce part of God's original plan for mankind? _____

5. What is the Biblical grounds for divorce? _____

6. Can divorce and remarriage be forgiven? _____

7. Where do we find in Scripture the Biblical pattern for a virtuous wife and mother? _____

8. What was the difference in Martha and Mary in light of the scripture found in Luke 10:38-42?

_____

_____

9. Are older women past the age of working for the Lord?

_____

10. What was Paul stressing in regard to the way women are to dress?

_____

Bibliography

Chilcote, Paul W. She Offered Them Christ (Nashville: Abingdon Press, 1993).

Deen, Edith. All of the Women of the Bible (New York: Harper & Row, Publishers, 1955).

Giles, Kevin. Patterns of Ministry Among the First Christians (Melbourne: Collins Dove, 1989).

Hagin, Kenneth E. The Woman Question (Greensburg: Manna Christian Outreach, 1975).

Hamon, Dr. Bill. Prophets Pitfalls and Principles (Shippensburg: Destiny Image, 1991).

Justice, Nancy. "Women Pastors Gain Acceptance," Charisma & Christian Life (Lake Mary: Strang Communications Co., July 1993, Vol. 18, No. 12).

Keener, Craig S. ... And Marries Another (Peabody: Hendrikson Publishers, 1991).

Sitton, Maryann. Hey Woman, Be Quiet (Hamilton, MT: Shiloh Christian Retreat, 1973).

Trombley, Charles. Who Says Women Can't Teach? (South Plainfield: Bridge Publishing Inc., 1985).

Neither Male Nor Female

What You Need to Know About
Christ Unlimited Ministries

Purpose and Vision

Go ye therefore, and teach all nations, baptizing them in the name of the Father, and of the Son, and of the Holy Ghost: Teaching them to observe all things whatsoever I have commanded you: and, lo, I am with you alway, even unto the end of the world. Amen

Matthew 28:19,20

CHRIST UNLIMITED is not "another denomination," sect, or just a separate group. It is an arm of the Body of Christ — the Church of Jesus Christ, which has been called to strengthen the Body at large. We also believe we have been called to help establish the Kingdom of God in the earth.

CHRIST UNLIMITED is open to help and work with all Bible-believing Christians regardless of their church or denominational affiliations and committed to helping wherever possible in evangelistic and teaching outreaches.

CHRIST UNLIMITED believes that time is running out and the Gospel has not been preached to every creature. Many nations have not heard the Gospel, and in many places, doors for evangelism are closing. We believe it is time all Christians cooperated with the Lord in breaking down denominational walls for a united front line against the kingdom of darkness and in setting up the Kingdom of the Lord Jesus Christ by the power of the Holy Spirit.

CHRIST UNLIMITED provides such tools as to enable the saints of God to establish the Kingdom of God in the earth. We encourage groups of prayer warriors who will pray, fast, and intercede for the nations. This, we believe, is weapon number one. We teach believers how to overcome through spiritual warfare and through knowing how to use their authority in Christ Jesus through the Word and the power of the Holy Spirit.

Christians need to know how to bring down the forces of darkness in their own lives and in the lives of those to whom they minister. We provide such tools as Bibles, literature, CHRIST UNLIMITED books, and cassettes. We promote the Gospel going out by any means of communication, including the INTERNET, radio and video, as well as literature. We promote teaching seminars, Bible schools, and correspondence courses, all aimed at winning souls to Christ and building the Body of Christ into maturity.

Bud and Betty Miller serve the Lord together as founders of the multi-visioned ministry outreach, CHRIST UNLIMITED. The outreaches of this ministry have stemmed from a tremendous desire to see the Word of God taught in its balanced entirety. The Millers are firm believers in prayer and, through prayer, have seen many released from the bondages of fear, failure, and defeat.

Christ Unlimited — P.O. Box 850 — Dewey, AZ 86327   USA

The Millers have a world-wide vision for spreading the full-gospel message and teaching God's Word. Bud not only preaches and pastors a church, but is director of **CHRIST UNLIMITED PUBLISHING**, an outreach dedicated to publishing God's Word in many languages. His experience, openness to the Holy Spirit, and down-to-earth expression of God's love have blessed many. God has endowed Betty with a rare gift of teaching that makes her a practical and effective "handmaiden of the Lord." Both Bud and Betty have hearts turned toward evangelism and missions, desiring to tell everyone of God's wonderful love. Their anointed teaching comes across with simplicity and in the power of the Holy Spirit.

The outreaches of **CHRIST UNLIMITED** are in obedience to the words of our Lord in Mark 16:15: Go ye into all the world and preach the gospel to every creature. This mandate from the Lord presents a challenge to our generation as an estimated 25 percent of the world's population still have not heard the Good News of Jesus Christ.[1]

CHRIST UNLIMITED MINISTRIES also is dedicated to teaching God's Word. Hosea 4:6 says: My people are destroyed for lack of knowledge. Many Christians are leading defeated lives simply because they do not know God's Word in its fullest.

CHRIST UNLIMITED MINISTRIES has provided literature for those who desire to know God's Word in a greater way. The main thrust of the teaching and literature is directed at "How to be an overcomer." In the endtimes, we must be prepared to overcome the onslaughts of Satan. Many Christians are suffering needlessly, because they do not know how to overcome sickness, depression, divorce, fear, and financial failure. **CHRIST UNLIMITED MINISTRIES** provides answers for troubled families as well as trains workers for service.

DOCTRINAL STATEMENT

> Jesus answered them, and said, My doctrine is not mine, but his that sent me. If any man will do his will, he shall know of the doctrine, whether it be of God, or whether I speak of myself
>
> John 7:16,17

Inspiration of Scriptures: We believe that the Holy Bible is the written Word of the Living God. We believe it was inspired by the Holy Spirit and recorded by holy men of old. It is infallible in content and a perfect treasure of heavenly instruction which is truth without any mixture of error. The Bible reveals the principles by which God will judge us and reveals His great plan of salvation. It will remain eternally. We believe the Bible is the true center of Christian union and the supreme standard by which all human conduct, creeds, and opinions should be tried. Therefore, we believe this Word should go into all the world and should be given first place in every believer's life (2 Tim. 3:16; Heb. 4:12; 1 Pet. 1:23-25; and 2 Pet. 1:19-21).

God: We believe in one God revealed in three persons: the Father, the Son, and the Holy Ghost . . . making up the blessed Trinity (Matt. 3:16,17; 1 John 5:6,7).

Man: We believe that man, in his natural state, is a sinner — lost, undone, without hope, and without God (Rom. 3:19-23; Gal. 3:22; Eph. 2:1,2,12).

Salvation: We believe the terms of salvation are repentance toward God for sin and a personal, heartfelt faith in the Lord Jesus Christ. This will result in a new birth. Salvation is possible only through God's grace, not by our works. Works are simply the fruit of salvation (Acts 3:19,20; Rom. 4:1-5; 5:1; Eph. 2:8-10).

Body of Christ: We believe the Body of Christ is made up of all who have been born again regardless of denominational differences. We believe in the spirit of unity, while allowing for variety in individual ministries as to their work, calling, and location as directed by the Holy Spirit (Acts 10:34,35; 1 Cor. 12:12-31).

Blood Atonement: We believe in the saving power of the blood of Jesus and His imputed righteousness (Acts 4:12; Rom. 4:1-9; 5:1-11; Eph. 1:3-14).

Bodily Resurrection: We believe in the bodily resurrection of Jesus Christ (Luke 24:39-43; John 20:24-29).

Ascension: We believe that Christ Jesus ascended to the Father and is presently engaged in building a place for us in His Kingdom and interceding for the saints (John 14:2,3; Rom. 8:34).

Second Coming: We believe in the visible, bodily return of Christ Jesus to this earth, to meet His Church (Bride) and to judge the world (Acts 1:10,11; 1 Thess. 4:13-18; 2 Thess. 1:7-10; James 5:8; Rev. 1:7).

Ordinances: We believe that the two ordinances of the Body of Christ are water baptism and the Lord's Supper (Matt. 28:19; 1 Cor. 11:24-26).

Heaven and Hell: We believe Scripture clearly sets forth the doctrines of eternal punishment for the lost and eternal bliss and service for the saved — a literal hell for the unsaved and heaven for the saved (Matt. 25:34,41,46; Luke 16:19-31; John 14:1-3; Rev. 20:11-15).

Holy Spirit: We believe the Holy Spirit to be the third person of the Trinity whose purpose in the redemption of man is to convict of sin, regenerate the repentant believer, guide the believer into all truth, indwell all believers, and give gifts to those He wills that they may minister as Christ would to men. We believe that the manifestations of the Holy Spirit recorded in 1 Corinthians 12:1-11 will operate through present-day Christians who yield to Jesus (Luke 11:13; John 7:37-39; 14:16,17; 16:7-14; Acts 2:1-18).

We believe the baptism in the Holy Spirit, with the evidence of speaking in other tongues as the Spirit gives utterance, is for all believers as promised by John the Baptist (Matt. 3:11), Jesus (Acts 1:4-8), and Peter (Acts 2:38-41). The fulfillment of this promise was witnessed by early disciples of Christ (Acts 2:4; 10:44-47; 19:1-6) and operates in many present-day disciples of the Lord Jesus Christ.

Christ Unlimited — P.O. Box 850 — Dewey, AZ 86327   USA

Divine Healing: We believe God has used doctors, medicines, and other natural means of healing; however, we believe divine healing is provided for believers in the atonement made by Jesus' blood shed on the cross (Isa. 53:5; 1 Pet. 2:24). We believe divine healing may be appropriated by the laying on of hands by the elders (James 5:14-16), by the prayer of an anointed person gifted by the Holy Spirit for healing the sick (1 Cor. 12:9), or by a direct act of receiving this provision by faith (Mark 11:23,24)

MINISTRY FINANCING

But seek ye first the kingdom of God, and his righteousness; and all these things shall be added unto you.
Matthew 6:33

We want to share with readers the instructions the Lord gave us in regard to financing this ministry. As this is the Holy Spirit's work, we are to let Him speak to the hearts of people as to what and how much He wants them to give. Quite simply, we are to share the vision He has given us and trust Him to provide for all that we need. We believe the Lord pays for the things He orders, and if He does not order something, we do not want to engage in it. Pray with us that we will stay close to the Lord, and that, in seeking His righteousness, we will be able to hear His instructions clearly as to what He desires us to do. If we do that, we know we shall never lack of the things needed to do His work.

CHRIST UNLIMITED MINISTRIES, INC. is a 501(c)(3) tax-exempt, non-profit church, established locally in the Prescott Valley, Arizona, area.

'Barrett, David B. Cosmos, Chaos, and Gospel (Birmingham: New Hope Publishers, 1987), p. 75.

Christ Unlimited — P.O. Box 850 — Dewey, AZ 86327   USA

FOR ADDITIONAL STUDY

This book is taken from a course of Bible studies called the Overcoming Life Series. The entire series is a virtual "spiritual tool chest," as it covers a multitude of subjects every Christian faces in his walk with God. It also answers questions that many believers have concerning the current move of God. These are dealt with in a balanced approach and in the light of the Scripture. God's people are not to live frustrated, defeated lives, but rather they are to be victorious overcomers! Other books available with their companion workbooks are:

PROVE ALL THINGS - Christ warned that great deception would be one of the signs of the end times. In this book, instruction is given on how to recognize false prophets and teachings. Clear Scriptural guidelines are given on discerning the Spirit of truth versus the spirit of error. The book deals with how to judge without being judgmental.

THE TRUE GOD - This is a teaching on the character of God, explaining why God does certain things, and why it is against His nature to do other things. It differentiates between the things for which God is responsible and the things for which the devil is responsible. Our responsibility as Christians destined to overcome is made clear so that we can live victorious lives.

THE WILL OF GOD - This lesson teaches us not only how to know the will of God in our personal lives, family, ministry and finances, but also brings understanding as to why God allows sin, sickness and suffering in the world. As overcomers, Christians are not to suffer under many of the things we have accepted as normal.

KEYS TO THE KINGDOM - Instruction on how to gain authority in God's Kingdom through prayer is the topic of this book. Many principles and methods of prayer are covered, such as praying in the Spirit, fasting and prayer, travailing prayer, praise, intercession and spiritual warfare.

EXPOSING SATAN'S DEVICES - This book is a powerful expose' of Satan's tricks, tactics and lies. Cult and Occultic methods and groups are listed so Christians can detect their activity. Demon activity is discussed and deliverance and casting out demons is dealt with in detail. Satan's kingdom is uncovered and the Christian is taught to overcome through spiritual discernment and warfare.

HEALING OF THE SPIRIT, SOUL AND BODY - This book teaches how to overcome emotional problems, as well as physical ones, and how to receive divine healing. It also teaches how to renew the carnal mind and walk in the spirit of life, thereby overcoming depression, loneliness and fear.

NEITHER MALE NOR FEMALE - What is the woman's role in the church and home? Who is a woman's spiritual head and covering? Does God call women to the fivefold ministry? What does God's Word say about divorce, celibacy and choosing a marriage partner? These and other woman related topics are Scripturally examined.

EXTREMES OR BALANCE? - Many Christians have hurt the cause of Christ through "out-of-balance" teachings and demonstrations. This book shows how to avoid those areas. It also deals wisely with the excesses and extremes in the body of Christ.

THE PATHWAY INTO THE OVERCOMER'S WALK - This book contains answers to the questions an overcomer faces as he presses toward the prize of the high calling in Christ Jesus. How can we be conformed to the image of Christ? How does the Holy Spirit work with the overcomers in the end times? What are the overcomer's rewards?

Please visit our website for information on how to order the complete "Overcoming Life Bible Study."   www.Bible.com

Christ Unlimited — P.O. Box 850 — Dewey, AZ 86327   USA

.

Neither Male Nor Female Workbook

Answers to Lesson and Quiz

Christ Unlimited — P.O. Box 850 — Dewey, AZ 86327   USA

Answers to Lesson, Section One

I. **The Role of Women in General**
   A 1. Counterfeit
      2. After the fall of Adam and Eve, or when they sinned
   B. Men and women
      1. Female
      2. Sin (or fall, or disobedience)
   C. Gender (or sex)
   D. Submitted
      1. Head
      2. Submission, preferring one another, or love

II. **Attitudes of Submission**
   A. Jesus (or Christ, or the Lord)
      1. When something is against God's Word or His will
      2. God
         a. Abigail
         b. Sapphira
      3. Jesus
         a. Household or family
         b. Rahab
   B. 1. Rebelling
      2. Any, or every
      3. Leadership

III. **The Reason for Authority and Submission**
   A. Order
      1. Example
      2. Obey
   B. Subject, or submissive
      1. Elders or older ones
      2. Accusation

Christ Unlimited — P.O. Box 850 — Dewey, AZ 86327   USA

Answers to Review Outline Quiz, Section One

1. The Bible, or the Word of God
2. Jesus Christ, or being born again
3. Male — female
4. Obedience — faithfulness or submissiveness
5. The right condition of the heart
6. Jesus, the Holy Spirit, or God (any or all are correct)
7. Jesus as Head of the Church
8. Willingness, agreeableness — force, resignation
9. Correction
10. Love and example

Christ Unlimited — P.O. Box 850 — Dewey, AZ 86327   USA

Answers to Lesson, Section Two

I. The Gifts of Jesus to the Church
   A. Gifts
      1. Five-fold
         a. Apostles
         b. Prophets
         c. Evangelists
         d. Pastors
         e. Teachers
      2. Ordained
      3. Sex, or gender

   B. Maturity, perfection, or fullness of God
      1. Apostle
         a. "A sent one" or "one sent forth"
         b. Miracles, signs, and wonders or mighty deeds
         c. Ordain
         d. The 12 disciples and Paul and Junia
      2. Prophet
         a. Divine utterances
         b. Women
            1) Miriam
            2) Huldah
            3) Deborah
            4) Anna
            5) Philip's daughters
      3. Evangelist
         a. To fulfill the Great Commission
         b. Mark, Barnabas, and Philip
      4. Pastor
         a. "To feed and take care of"
         b. To be a steward or overseer over the flock that belongs to God and
            to feed them
      5. Teacher
         a. Revelation
         b. Expound or teach
   C. 500
         2. Presbyterian — the elders rule
         3. Congregational — the congregation rules
         4. Independent — the pastor rules with an advisory board

II. Role of Women in the Five-fold Ministry
   A. Men — women
      1. Equal in God's image
      2. New
   B. Body
      1. No
      2. Order in congregational and public services
      3. Not if they truly have been called and ordained by Jesus
         a. Jesus'
         b. Phoebe and Priscilla
          c. Junia

Answers to Review Outline Quiz, Section Two

1. Yes
2. No
3. Because he mentions a number of women in ministries and does not condemn them or the local assemblies where they serve
4. Disorder in public assemblies
5. Yes
6. Deborah
7. Yes
8. Priscilla
9. To a greater extent than heretofore, but still not by the majority of Christian churches or denominations
10. Assemblies of God

Christ Unlimited — P.O. Box 850 — Dewey, AZ 86327   USA

Answers to Lesson, Section Three

I. Women's Problems in the Home and Ministry
   A. 1. Custom or tradition
      2. Hair
         a. Husband
         b. Christ or Jesus
      3. Spiritual
      4. Jesus or Christ
         a. Mourning
         b. Shameful or dishonoring
         c. Light
      5. Cover
         a. Mouths, or conversations
         b. Prayers

II. Paul's Advice to Women About Marriage
   A. Single, or celibate
      1. Advice, belief, suggestion, opinion, or judgment
      2. He is put in first place
         a. Choice — commitment
         b. Believer, or born again person
         c. Holy Spirit
   B. Sanctified or saved
      1. Depart, leave, or go
      2. Bodies or sex life
         a. For a specific purpose, such as fasting and special prayer
         b. Agreement
         c. Satan would not be able to tempt them
   C. Sin, or wrong, or sinful
      1. Divorce, or putting away
      2. Covered under the blood of Jesus, as far as the East is from the West, remembered no more, erased, forgotten
      3. Repented
         a. Yes
         b. Rebellion, or disobedience, or licentiousness, premeditated sin
      4. No
         1. He meant a church leader could not be presently living in polygamy (having more than one wife at a time).
         2. Dress, or apparel, or appearance

Christ Unlimited — P.O. Box 850 — Dewey, AZ 86327   USA

III. The Ideal Woman in Scripture
  A. Yes
      1. At a job, or having a career
      2. Fearing the Lord
      3. Her husband and children, or her family
  B. Obedience, or response
  C. Help them